GOD'S ANSWERS TO LIFE'S DIFFICULT QUESTIONS

Books by Rick Warren

The Purpose Driven® Life

The Purpose Driven® Church

Rick Warren's Bible Study Methods

What on Earth Am I Here For?

Living with Purpose Series

God's Answers to Life's Difficult Questions

God's Power to Change Your Life

LIVING WITH PURPOSE

RICK WARREN

GOD'S ANSWERS TO LIFE'S DIFFICULT QUESTIONS

ZONDERVAN®

GRAND RAPIDS, MICHIGAN 49530 USA

ZONDERVAN.COM/
AUTHORTRACKER

ZONDERVAN®

God's Answers to Life's Difficult Questions
Copyright © 2006 by Rick Warren
Previously titled *Answers to Life's Most Difficult Questions*

Requests for information should be addressed to:

Zondervan, *Grand Rapids, Michigan 49530*

ISBN-10: 0-310-27393-5
ISBN-13: 978-0-310-27393-6

International Trade Paper Edition

Interior design by Beth Shagene

Printed in the United States of America

07 08 09 10 • 16 15 14 13 12 11 10 9 8 7 6 5 4 3

I dedicate this book to my flock,
the members of Saddleback Valley
Community Church.
They have an insatiable hunger for
practical teaching from God's Word,
listen intently,
and seek to apply the truth to their lives.
I am grateful to be their pastor.

Contents

PREFACE

Many books today focus on self-improvement. Everyone wants to change for the better. Americans will spend millions of dollars this year in their search for practical solutions to their problems. Many will move from one fad to another, looking for advice on how to live and for answers to perplexing questions.

Unfortunately, much of the advice being dispensed through television, radio, and print these days is highly unreliable. It is based on popular opinion and current thinking. Therein lies a problem, because today's "pop psychology" will be discarded next year for a new approach or therapy.

Jesus said, "You will know the truth, and the truth will set you free!" Lasting freedom from personal hang-ups comes from building our lives on the truth. Only the Bible can be depended on completely to provide truthful insights into the causes and cures for our personal problems. God's Word has stood the test of time. It is just as relevant and applicable today as it was thousands of years ago. It contains the answers to life's most difficult questions.

However, it is not enough to simply *say*, "The Bible is the answer." It is important for Christians to *show how* the Bible answers life's questions. In this book I suggest practical steps and specific actions you can take, based on God's Word, that will help you cope with the common problems we all face. The great evangelist D. L. Moody once said, "The Bible was not given to increase our knowledge, but to change our lives."

When Jesus taught, his intention was that those who listened would "go and do likewise." He aimed for specific actions and commitments. In each of these twelve studies you will discover simple ways to apply God's truth to your personal life, your family, other relationships, and your job. The way to get the most out of this book is to act on it!

Why are there so many biographical stories in the Bible? The apostle Paul said, "Everything that was written in the past was written to teach us, so that through endurance and encouragement of the Scriptures we might have hope" (Rom. 15:4). God gave us these examples from people's lives for two reasons.

First, they are given to teach us. It is always wise to learn from our own experiences, but it is even wiser to learn from the experiences of others. It is usually less painful too! By applying the principles illustrated in the lives of Bible characters, we can avoid making some of the same costly mistakes they made.

Second, God gave us these stories to encourage us. We are encouraged by the fact that he chooses to use ordinary people to accomplish his plans—in spite of their weaknesses and failures and sometimes mixed motives. That gives us hope that God can work in our lives also!

It is my prayer that these studies of Bible characters will produce two results in your life: that you will learn God's principles for successful living, and that you will believe God can use you in a significant way.

CHAPTER 1

How Can I Cope with Stress?

J esus Christ was constantly under pressure. There were grueling demands on his time; he rarely had any personal privacy; he was constantly interrupted. People repeatedly misunderstood him, criticized him, and ridiculed him. He had enormous stress, which would have caused any of us to cave in.

But as we look at the life of Christ, we quickly discover that he remained at peace under pressure. He was never in a hurry. He was always at ease. He had a calmness about his life that enabled him to handle enormous amounts of stress. How did he do this so successfully? The answer can be simply stated: he based his life on sound principles of stress management. If we understand and apply these eight principles in our lives, we will experience less pressure and more peace of mind.

IDENTIFICATION: KNOW WHO YOU ARE

Jesus said, "I am the light of the world. Whoever follows me will never walk in darkness, but will have the light of life" (John 8:12). "I am the door" (10:9 KJV); "I am the way and the truth and the life" (14:6); "I am the good shepherd" (10:11); "I am God's Son" (10:36). Christ knew who he was!

The first principle for handling stress in your life is this: *Know who you are.* It is the principle of identification. Jesus said, "I know who I am. I testify for myself" (see John 8:18). This is critically important in stress management because if you don't know who you are, someone else may try to tell you who *they* think you are. If you don't know who you are, you will subconsciously let other people manipulate you and pressure you into believing you are somebody you aren't.

A lot of stress in life results from our hiding behind masks, living double lives, being unreal with others, or trying to be somebody we're not. Insecurity always produces pressure in our lives, and when we are insecure, we feel coerced to perform and conform. We set unrealistic standards for our lives, and even though we work, work, work, we still can't meet those unrealistic standards. Tension and pressure naturally occur as a result.

The first way to balance stress in my life is to get an internal balance of who I am. And I know *who* I am by knowing *whose* I am. I am a child of God. I was put on earth not by accident, but for a purpose. I am deeply loved by God. I am accepted by him. He has a plan for my life, and because he put me here, I am significant.

And because he put *you* here, *you* are significant. To handle stress you must know who you are. Until you handle this issue, you will be hindered by insecurity.

DEDICATION: KNOW WHOM YOU'RE TRYING TO PLEASE

The second principle of stress management in the life of Christ is found in John 5:30: "By myself I can do nothing; I judge only as I hear, and my judgment is just, for I seek not to please myself but him who sent me."

The principle is this: *Know whom you're trying to please.* You can't please everybody, because by the time one group becomes pleased with you, another group gets upset with you. Even God doesn't please everybody, so it's foolish to try to do something that even God doesn't do!

Jesus knew whom he was trying to please; it was a settled issue with him: "I'm going to please God the Father." And the Father replied, "This is my beloved Son, in whom I am well pleased" (Matt. 3:17 KJV).

When you don't know whom you're trying to please, you cave in to three things: *criticism* (because you are concerned about what others will think of you), *competition* (because you worry about whether somebody else is getting ahead of you), and *conflict* (because you're threatened when anyone disagrees with you). If I "seek first the kingdom of God and his righteousness," then all the other necessary things of life will be added unto me (Matt. 6:33 KJV). This means that if I focus on pleasing God, it will simplify my life. I will always be doing the right thing—the thing that pleases God—regardless of what anybody else thinks.

We love to blame our stress on other people and obligations: "You *made* me … I *have* to … I've *got* to." Actually, there are few things in life (apart from our jobs) that we *must* do. When we say, "I have to, I must, I've got to," we may really be saying, "I choose to, because I don't want to pay the consequences." Hardly anybody *makes* us do anything, so usually we can't blame other people for our stress. When we feel pressure, we are *choosing* to allow other people to put us under pressure. We are not victims unless we *allow* ourselves to be pressured by other people's demands.

ORGANIZATION: KNOW WHAT YOU'RE TRYING TO ACCOMPLISH

Here is Christ's clue to the third principle for dealing with stress: "Even if I testify on my own behalf, my testimony is valid, for I know where I came from and where I am going" (John 8:14). The principle is this: *Know what you want to accomplish.* Christ said, "I know where I came from, and I know where I'm going." Unless you plan your life and set priorities, you will be pressured by other people to do what they think is important.

Every day, either you live by priorities or you live by pressures. There is no other option. Either you decide what is important in your life, or you let other people decide what is important in your life.

It is easy to operate under the tyranny of the urgent, to come to the end of your day and think, "Have I really accomplished anything? I used a lot of energy and did a lot of things, but did I accomplish anything important?" Busyness is not necessarily productivity. You may be spinning in circles, but you're not accomplishing anything.

Preparation causes you to be at ease. To put it another way, preparation prevents pressure but procrastination produces it. Good organization and good preparation reduce stress because you know who you are, whom you're trying to please, and what you want to accomplish. *Having clear goals greatly simplifies life.* Spend a few minutes each day talking with God in prayer. Look at your schedule for the day and decide, "Is this really the way I want to spend a day of my life? Am I willing to exchange twenty-four hours of my life for these activities?"

Concentration: Focus on One Thing at a Time

Do you sometimes find yourself pulled in different directions? Several people tried to detour Jesus from his planned schedule. They tried to distract him from his goal in life. "At daybreak Jesus went out to a solitary place. The people were looking for him and when they came to where he was, they tried to keep him from leaving them" (Luke 4:42). Jesus was going to leave, but they tried to make him stay.

Jesus responded, "I must preach the good news of the kingdom of God to the other towns also, because that is why I was sent" (v. 43). He refused to be distracted by less important matters.

Principle number four for stress management is this: *Focus on one thing at a time.* It is the principle of concentration. Jesus was a master at this. It seemed that everybody tried to interrupt him; everyone had a Plan B for him. But Jesus responded, "Sorry, I must keep on moving toward my goal." He kept right on doing what he knew God had told him to do: preach about the kingdom of God. He was determined. He was persistent. He was focused.

When I have thirty things to do on my desk, I clear my desk and work on one thing. When I finish that, I pick up something else. You can't catch two jackrabbits at once. You've got to focus on one.

When we diffuse our efforts, we are ineffective. When we concentrate our efforts, we are more effective. Light diffused produces a hazy glow, but light concentrated produces fire. Jesus Christ did not let interruptions prevent him from concentrating on his goal; he did not let others make him tense or stressed or irritated.

Delegation: Don't Do It All Yourself

One day "Jesus went up on a mountainside and called to him those he wanted, and they came to him" (Mark 3:13). He appointed twelve men, whom he designated as apostles, so they might be with him and he could send them out to preach. In other words, Jesus delegated his authority. This is the fifth principle: *Don't try to do it all yourself.* Use the principle of delegation.

Do you know why we get uptight and tense? Because we think everything depends on us. "Here I am—Atlas—holding up the cares of the world. They're all on my shoulders. If I happen to let go, the world will fall apart." But when I really do let go, the world doesn't fall apart! Jesus enlisted and trained twelve disciples so that they could share his load. He delegated his work. He got other people involved.

Why don't we delegate? Why don't we get other people involved? Why do we try to do it all ourselves? For two reasons. The first reason is *perfectionism*. We think, "If I want a job well done, I'll do it myself." That's a nice idea, but often it doesn't work well because there are just too many things to be done. We simply don't have time to do everything ourselves. It's really an egotistical attitude that says, "Nobody, but nobody, can do it the way I can."

Do you think Jesus would have done a better job than these disciples? Of course he would have. But he let them do the work even though he would have done it better. We need to let other people make some of the mistakes so that they can learn, the way the disciples did. Don't rob others of an education!

The other reason we don't delegate is personal *insecurity*. "What if I turn over this responsibility to someone, and he does a better job at it?" That thought is threatening to us. But you won't be threatened by that possibility if you know who you are, whom you're trying to please, what you want to accomplish, and what one thing you want to focus on. In order to be effective, you *must* get other people involved, because you can't focus on more than one thing at a time and do it effectively.

MEDITATION: MAKE A HABIT OF PERSONAL PRAYER

Jesus often got up "very early in the morning, while it was still dark, . . . and went off to a solitary place" to pray (Mark 1:35). The sixth principle of stress management is, *Make a habit of personal prayer.* This is the principle of meditation. *Prayer is a gigantic stress-reliever.* It is a God-given tool for letting off your anxieties. No matter how busy Jesus got, he made it a practice to spend time alone with God. If Jesus made time for prayer when he was busy, how much more do you and I need prayer! A little quiet time alone with God can be a decompression chamber for life's stresses. We talk with God in prayer; we tell him what's on our minds and let him talk to us as we read the Bible. Then we look at our schedules, evaluate our priorities, and wait for instructions. (In my book *Rick Warren's Bible Study Methods* there is a detailed explanation of how to develop and continue the habit of a daily devotional time with God.)

Many of our problems come from our inability to sit still. We just don't know how to be quiet. Most of us cannot sit in a car for five minutes without turning the radio on.

If you walk into your house and find that you're all alone, what's the first thing you do? You probably turn on the TV or a music CD. Silence makes us uncomfortable. But God says, "Be still, and know that I am God" (Ps. 46:10). One reason many people don't know God personally is that they can't be still. They're too busy to be quiet and just think.

Someone once said, "It seems to be an ironic habit of man that when he loses his way he doubles his speed"—like an Air Force pilot in World War II who flew out over the Pacific. When he radioed in, the controller asked, "Where are you?" The pilot replied, "I don't know, but I'm making record time!"

A lot of people are like that: they are speeding through life, but they don't know where they are headed. We need to start our morning with prayer, as Jesus did, and then periodically through the day stop and pray again, to recharge our spiritual batteries.

Recreation: Take Time Off to Enjoy Life

Once Jesus' twelve men gathered around him and reported all that they had done and taught. "Because so many people were coming and going that they did not even have a chance to eat, he said to them, 'Come with me by yourselves to a quiet place and get some rest'" (Mark 6:31). Principle number seven for stress management is, *Take time off to enjoy life.* It's the principle of relaxation and recreation. Jesus looked at these men who had been working hard without relief and said, "You deserve a break today. Let's get some rest. Let's take some time off." So they got into a boat, rowed to the other side of the lake, and went out to the desert to rest.

One reason why Jesus could handle stress is that he knew when to relax. He frequently went to either the mountains or the desert just to unwind.

Rest and recreation in life are not optional. In fact, rest is so important that God included it in the Ten Commandments. The Sabbath was made for mankind because God knows that our physical, emotional, and spiritual constitutions demand periodic breaks. Jesus survived stress because he enjoyed life. One of my favorite verses, Matthew 11:19 in the Phillips paraphrase, says that Jesus came "enjoying life." Paul wrote that God has richly provided "everything for our enjoyment" (1 Tim. 6:17). Balance in life is a key to stress management.

TRANSFORMATION: GIVE YOUR STRESS TO CHRIST

The eighth principle of stress management is one that Jesus didn't need because he is the Son of God, but that we need because we're merely human. Jesus says, "Come to me, all you who are weary and burdened, and I will give you rest. Take my yoke upon you and learn from me, for I am gentle and humble in heart, and you will find rest for your souls. For my yoke is easy and my burden is light" (Matt. 11:28–30). So the final principle of stress management is, *Give your stress to Christ.* You will never enjoy complete peace of mind until you have a relationship with the Prince of Peace.

Christ did *not* say, "Come to me and I will give you more guilt, more burdens, more stress, and more worries"—even though that's what a lot of people seem to teach! Some churches tend to create pressure rather than relieve it. But Jesus said, "I want to give you *rest.* I am the Stress-Reliever. When you get in harmony with me, I will give you inner strength."

Christ can transform your lifestyle from stressful to satisfied. The greatest source of stress comes from trying to live our lives apart from the God who made us, trying to go our own way and be our own god.

What do you need? If you have never committed your life to Christ, you need a transformation. Give your life, with all its stresses, to him and say, "Lord, please give me a new life. Replace the pressure I feel with the peace you offer. Help me follow your principles of stress management."

PUTTING THOUGHTS INTO ACTION

1. Which two or three of the eight principles stand out as the ones you most need to deal with right now?
2. Identify three specific ways you can begin to simplify your life within the next week.

CHAPTER 2

HOW CAN I REBOUND
FROM FAILURE?

We all make mistakes, and sometimes they are pretty bad. But a failure can become a stepping-stone to success. An incident from Peter's life (Luke 5:1–11) illustrates this wonderful truth. One time Peter and his friends had been out fishing all night, but they had caught nothing. This was probably unusual, since Peter was a professional fisherman. He was definitely not a novice. He probably had the best nets, owned a good boat, and knew exactly where to catch the most fish. He had worked all night, as his income depended on a good catch. Still, Peter came up short. Even superstars strike out sometimes.

The next day, the fishermen were washing their nets on the seashore, feeling very tired and discouraged. At that moment Jesus came along and said, "Peter, I'd like to use your boat as a platform for a speech." So Peter let Jesus into his boat, and they launched out a little way from the shore. There Jesus could speak from the boat to the crowd standing on the shore.

After finishing his message, Jesus said to the fishermen, "Now let's go fishing. Launch out into the deep water, and let down the nets for a catch."

Peter replied, "Master, we've worked hard all night and haven't caught anything. But because you say so, I'll let down the nets." When the disciples obeyed, they caught such a large number of fish that their nets began to break.

WHEN OUR BEST IS NOT ENOUGH

What does this story teach us about failure? Jesus never performed a miracle without a purpose. He always used his miracles to illustrate principles. This incident teaches us what to do when our best is not good enough.

Sometimes we give something our best shot but still come up ten feet short. We study diligently for a test and only get a "C," or we work hard to make our marriage better but still don't see any progress. Life can be tough at times, and it's tempting to give up. We feel like saying, "What's the use? I just set myself up for more failure. Can anything make a difference?"

The interesting part of the Bible story is the comparison between the two catches. The disciples had worked all night and caught nothing, but later they went out again for ten minutes and caught more than they ever had before. It was the same lake, the same boat, the same nets, and the same people fishing. So what made the difference?

There are actually three differences between the two fishing expeditions, and these differences give us principles to follow when our best attempts end in failure. I believe any person who applies these principles will be a genuine success in life. God intended them to be easy to understand, so that everybody could get in on the benefit.

But first you must realize that God *is interested* in your success; he's not interested in seeing you fail. Suppose my daughter Amy said to me one day, "Dad, I'm a total failure in life. Everything I touch falls apart. My problems are insurmountable. I can never do anything right. I'm a total failure and I'll never change."

Would I reply, "Oh, I'm so happy you told me that! That makes me feel so good inside"? Of course not. As a father, I want my children to be successful, to be the best they can be. Likewise, your heavenly Father wants you to be successful in life—in your personal life, your family, your spiritual growth, and all your relationships. There are three principles drawn from God's Word that can help you achieve this.

APPROPRIATE GOD'S PRESENCE IN YOUR LIFE

A clue to the first principle of success is found in Luke 5:3: Jesus was in the boat with the disciples. Christ's presence made a big difference! This time the disciples weren't fishing by themselves; God was with them. The first principle for successful living is this: *You must appropriate God's presence in your life.* In other words, you have to get Jesus into your boat. That's the starting point. Nothing has greater influence on your personal success than whether or not you are living with Christ in your life. For Peter, his boat represented his livelihood. When you're a fisherman, that boat is your business! It's significant that Peter made his boat available for Jesus to use. *Christ used Peter's business as a platform for ministry.*

Does God have access to your job? Is your business available for him to use at any time? Is he able to minister to people through your job? Too often we try to separate the secular and the spiritual; we have our Christian life nicely partitioned off from our career. But this prevents God from blessing your business or job. And the truth is, God will bless anything you give him. If you give him all your life, he will bless all of it. But if you give him just a part of it, he will bless just that one part.

A friend told me that as the president of his corporation he invites God to every board meeting. He reports that as a result, the board members make fewer mistakes and have more peace of mind about difficult decisions.

There is something about having Jesus in your boat that eliminates the fear of failure and reduces your worries about the results. When Peter made Christ his fishing partner, the results were incredible: he caught more fish than he had ever caught on his own. Don't miss the sequence, though. First Peter used his boat *for Christ's purposes.* Jesus took the boat and preached from it to reach people. Then, after Christ had used the boat for his own purposes, God took care of Peter's needs.

God promises us that if we "Seek ... first the kingdom of God, and his righteousness,... all these [other] things shall be added" unto us (Matt. 6:33 KJV). Does this mean that if I give my whole life to Christ, putting him first in every area, then he will bless it all? Yes, that is God's promise to you.

COOPERATE WITH GOD'S PLAN

The second principle is found in Luke 5:4. The second time the disciples went fishing, they fished under the direction of Christ, obediently following his instructions. We must not only appropriate God's presence in our lives, but also *cooperate with God's plan in our lives.* Jesus told the disciples where to fish, when to fish, and how to fish. *When God is guiding your life, you cannot fail.* As the late gospel singer Ethel Waters used to say, "God doesn't sponsor flops."

Peter's reaction to Christ's guidance was beautiful. First, he didn't argue. He didn't say, "Wait a minute, Jesus! I'm the premier professional fisherman on this lake. I own the record. Who are you to tell me how to fish?" He didn't ask, "Lord, are you sure?" He didn't ask any questions, and he also didn't hesitate. Peter might have been thinking that if he didn't catch anything at night, then he certainly wasn't going to catch anything in the middle of the day when the sun was glaring down on the water. But Peter didn't ask any questions; he just obeyed.

He also didn't listen to his feelings. I'm sure he was dog-tired from working all night, but he didn't ask, "What's the use? Why should I keep on going?" Peter's attitude was perfect. He was eager to cooperate with God's plan.

Why do you think Jesus said to Peter, "Launch out into the deep"? I think it was because it's in the deep water that the big fish are located. You only catch minnows in shallow water. Most people live in the shallow waters of life. They simply exist on a superficial level. There's little depth to their lives because they're content to just play around the edge, never getting out into deeper water. Why? Because it's safer in shallow water. They think, "If I get out into the deep water, there might be some waves. They might rock my boat, and it might overturn. So I'll just stay back here where it's safe and comfortable and fiddle around."

When God works in your life, it always involves risks, because God wants you to live by faith. Many Christians barely get their feet wet because they're afraid of getting in over their heads. They think, "If I really get serious about my commitment to the Lord, he may make me a fanatic. My family might get really upset. What will my friends think?" So they're content to live in the shallows of life—and they miss out on so much.

God's plan for your life is a good plan, one that will work for your benefit. God says, "Let me get into your boat. Let my presence be with you wherever you go—in your business, in your family, in your marriage, in every area. Let me direct you. Cooperate with my plan."

Anticipate God's Promises

The third principle is found in Luke 5:5: "Because you say so." To rebound from failure, you must *anticipate God's promises in your life.* In the second fishing attempt, the disciples were acting on the basis of God's promise to them. They went fishing again because they believed God would provide the fish. Now, Jesus didn't specifically say, "Peter, if you go fishing with me, I promise you'll make a big catch." He didn't need to say that, because Peter realized that when Christ told him to go fishing and also got into the boat and also told him exactly where to put down the net, it wasn't going to come up empty! Peter expected God to act. He expected God to keep his promise. Peter wasn't depending on his own fishing ability, so he wasn't afraid of failure. He believed in the promises of God.

When you get God's presence in your boat, and when you get God's plan in your head, and when you get God's promises in your heart, you cannot fail. Start expecting some wonderful results.

IT CAN WORK IN YOUR LIFE

Maybe you're saying, "That sounds great, but you don't know my circumstances. Right now I'm defeated by the problems I'm experiencing. I'm having some hard times." If you are feeling defeated by your circumstances, let me suggest an antidote for you. Read your Bible to find a specific promise from God, and then start claiming that promise. Start expecting God to act, and you will find that God's promise will inject new hope into a hopeless situation. Real success often begins at the point of failure.

I know a married couple who have had a severely damaged relationship, one that looked irreparable. But they sensed God saying to them, "I want you to stay together. Don't give up." Without any outward evidence they took on the same attitude that Peter did in his situation. They said, "Lord, we've worked on this marriage a long time, without improvement, but because you say so, we'll keep at it." Today they have a fulfilling marriage and a dynamic ministry together.

Look at the results when the disciples did what Jesus told them to do. "They caught such a large number of fish that their nets began to break" (Luke 5:6). God blessed them with more than they could handle. That is always the case when you appropriate God's presence, cooperate with God's plan, and anticipate God's promises—you will be blessed with more than you can handle. In fact, verse 7 points out that the disciples had to share the results with fishermen in another boat in order to keep from sinking. That's a great way to live!

The point is this: God not only wants to bless your life, but he wants to bless you so much that you have to share your blessing with others in order to keep yourself from sinking. He not only wants to bless *you*, but wants to bless *other people through you*—people whose nets are empty. God blessed the disciples with more than they could use for themselves.

The miracle so astounded Peter that he cried out, "Lord, I don't deserve this! I'm a sinner. This is too good for me."

Jesus then said to Peter, "Don't be afraid; from now on you will catch men" (v. 10). So the disciples beached their boats and left everything to follow Jesus.

The incident became a turning point in Peter's life and in the lives of the other disciples.

Think about what happened when the fishing party got to land. The disciples left their greatest catch ever sitting right there on the shore and went after Jesus! They realized that if Jesus could perform a miracle like that, he could do anything he wanted to. The disciples knew that as long as they followed him, their needs would be more than satisfied. Christ would take care of them no matter what happened. They wanted a relationship with him that was more than a one-time miracle. Then Christ invited them to become part of the greatest task in the world: "I'm going to make you fishers of men. You are going to share my Good News with other people."

Try It Again with Christ

How does this story relate to your life? Maybe you feel like the disciples before Christ came along: "I've worked all night and come up with an empty net." Does that describe your attitude toward your marriage, your job, or another personal problem? You feel that you haven't made any progress so you've said to yourself, "What's the use? Why keep on trying? Why put forth the effort?" Perhaps you have become a little cynical about life.

Peter didn't get cynical. He didn't say, "Lord, I've worked ten hours and didn't catch anything. That must mean there are no more fish in this lake." He knew that the fish were there—he just hadn't caught them yet.

Just because you haven't solved your problem doesn't mean a solution doesn't exist. It is often through failure that we learn the lessons that help us succeed. God's message to you is this: *Don't give up.* Try again, but this time do it with Jesus in your boat. He will make all the difference.

PUTTING THOUGHTS INTO ACTION

1. Focus on one specific problem in your life and, in a Bible study group or by using biblical aids such as a concordance, find some promises in the Bible that speak to an issue like this one.

2. What is your "boat" that God might want to use as a platform for his work?

CHAPTER 3

How Can I Defeat Depression?

Depression is one of the greatest problems in the world today. It has been called the common cold of emotional illnesses. Everyone gets depressed at times, but some people are depressed nearly all the time. And it's not limited to poor people or people with physical ailments. Even great saints get depressed. Elijah was just such an example.

Elijah was a tremendous spokesman for God. For three years he had been God's mouthpiece to the nation of Israel. All kinds of miracles had taken place, and there was a spiritual awakening throughout his nation, which had been mired in the worship of pagan idols.

One person who did not like Elijah was Jezebel, the queen of Israel. A very wicked woman, Jezebel hated Elijah because he had so much influence as a spokesman for the real God. After Elijah performed one particularly great miracle — calling down fire onto the altar on Mount Carmel — Jezebel's husband, King Ahab, told her everything that Elijah had done. This made her so angry that she sent a message to Elijah, saying, "May the gods deal with me, be it ever so severely, if by this time tomorrow I do not make your life like that of one of them" (1 Kings 19:2). She was saying, "If I don't kill you within twenty-four hours, I'll be ready to kill myself."

Elijah, who had been fearless for three years, becomes frightened when one woman threatens his life, and he runs out to the desert and then gets depressed (vv. 3–5). He comes to a broom tree, sits down under it, and prays that he might die. "I have had enough, LORD.... Take my life; I am no better than my ancestors."

Depressed Like Elijah?

Elijah was a prime candidate for depression. He was physically tired, he was emotionally exhausted, and somebody had threatened his life. He was an emotional basket case at this point, with all kinds of problems: fear, resentment, guilt, anger, loneliness, and worry. But God says that "Elijah was a man just like us" (James 5:17). He had the same problems we do, and in this case he had a problem with depression.

Elijah was so depressed that he was ready to die. Why do we get ourselves into such emotional messes? Sometimes because of what happens to us, bad circumstances that occur in our lives. But more often because of *faulty thinking*. The fact is that *our emotions are caused by our thoughts*.

If you think in a negative way, you are going to feel depressed. Your emotions are caused by how you interpret life. If you look at life from a negative viewpoint, you're going to get down.

If you want to get rid of negative emotions, you have to change the way you think. The Bible says that you can be transformed by the *renewing of your mind* (Rom. 12:2). To overcome depression

45

you must get your incorrect attitudes about life corrected. That's why Jesus said that when you "know the truth ... the truth will set you free" (John 8:32). If you look at things from the right point of view, that goes a long way toward not being depressed. The only way you can change your mind and emotions is by changing the way you think. Let's look at some ways to do that.

PLAYING THE MENTAL GAMES

Focus on the Facts, Not on Your Feelings

Why did Elijah get depressed? Because he played four mental games that all of us play when we get depressed. The first one is found in 1 Kings 19:3–4: "Elijah was afraid and ran for his life.... He came to a broom tree [a kind of desert shrub], sat down under it and prayed that he might die." Then he said, in effect, "Lord, I've had enough! I don't want to put up with it anymore. I'm just wasting my life. I'm trying to be your servant, but nobody's doing what's right. I'm fed up! It's no use trying; I'm giving up."

What was his first mistake? The same mistake we make when we get depressed: *we focus on our feelings rather than on the facts.* That always happens when we're depressed. We focus on how we feel rather than on reality. Elijah felt like a failure because of one incident that frightened him. He thought to himself, "I'm such a coward—what am I doing running?" So because he *felt* like a failure, he assumed he *was* a failure.

This is called emotional reasoning, and it is destructive. It is the "I feel it, so it must be true" idea. Musicians, athletes, and TV stars—to name a few—know that often after a performance they feel as though they've flopped. Yet they also know that they must learn to ignore those feelings because *feelings aren't always true.* Feelings are not facts; they can be highly unreliable.

For instance, a few weeks after I had been married to Kay, I woke up one morning and said, "You know, honey, I just don't feel married."

She replied, "It doesn't matter, buddy. You are!"

I don't always feel close to God either, but this doesn't necessarily mean that I'm far away from him. I don't always feel like a Christian, but I am one. Feelings often lie, so when we focus on our feelings rather than on the facts, we are going to get into trouble. For instance, after we have made a mistake in one area, we tend to feel as if we are total failures in life. That's a misconception. Everyone is entitled to make mistakes, and we can fail in some areas without being a failure as a person.

Most psychologists believe that one key to health is to get your feelings out in the open. Become aware. Vent your feelings. Get them out. But that's not the complete answer, because feelings are unreliable. The Bible doesn't tell us to get in touch with our *feelings* but to get in touch with the *truth*, because it's the truth that sets us free (John 8:32).

Don't Compare Yourself with Others

The second mistake Elijah made is revealed in his prayer: "I have had enough, LORD.... Take my life; I am no better than my ancestors" (1 Kings 19:4). A second cause of depression is that *we start comparing ourselves with other people*. Most of us have fallen into the trap of thinking, "If I could just be like so-and-so, I'd be happy."

When we start comparing ourselves with other people, we are asking for trouble. The Bible says it is both unwise and harmful (2 Cor. 10:12). We should not compare ourselves with somebody else because everyone is unique. There is only one person that you can be, and that is you. If you are always trying to imitate other people and act like them, you are going to get depressed. You have to be honest with yourself and be who you are. That is all God wants. That is all he expects.

When we start comparing ourselves with other people, we fall into another trap: we tend to compare our weaknesses with other people's strengths, forgetting that those people are also weak in areas where we may be strong. Moreover, we try to motivate ourselves through criticism and condemnation. We do this by "should-ing" ourselves: "I *should* be able to be like that person. I *should* be able to act better. I *should* be able to accomplish it. I *should* be able to stop it"—as if whipping ourselves verbally is going to motivate us! Nagging doesn't work when we do it to another person, and nagging ourselves with self-criticism doesn't work either.

Don't Take False Blame

The third mistake Elijah made is that he blamed himself for negative events that were not his fault. Elijah said, "I have been very zealous for the LORD God Almighty. The Israelites have rejected your covenant, broken down your altars, and put your prophets to death with the sword" (1 Kings 19:10). He said, in effect, "I have worked hard for three years, but they're still not any closer to you. I have really tried, but they're still living the same way as before."

In his depression Elijah blamed himself for failing to change the nation, and he took it personally. A third mistake that causes depression is that *we take false blame*. When we do that, we will always become depressed. If we assume a responsibility that God never intended us to have, it is too heavy a burden.

If you are in the habit of helping people, you realize sooner or later that people do not always respond the way you would like them to, whether it's your children, your friends, your spouse, or people you work with. People react in many different ways. You can't assume responsibility for their responses.

God has given each of us a free will. When you assume responsibility for other people's decisions, you accept a burden that will only depress you. You can sometimes *influence* people, but you cannot *control* them. The final decision is theirs. Don't be depressed by something you cannot control.

Don't Exaggerate the Negative

The fourth mistake Elijah made is that *he exaggerated the negative*. He said, "I am the only one left, and now they are trying to kill me too" (v. 10). Elijah held a little pity party for himself: "Everybody's against me." But the fact is that almost nobody was against him. Only one person violently opposed him, and her threat wasn't a real threat. If Elijah had simply thought about the situation instead of listening only to his feelings, he would have realized that Jezebel didn't dare kill him. The queen did send a messenger with the threat of death. But if Jezebel had really intended to kill Elijah, she wouldn't have sent a messenger to warn him; she would have just sent a hit man!

Jezebel was too intelligent to have Elijah killed. She recognized his powerful influence over his fellow Israelites. If Elijah had been killed, he would have become a martyr. That would have increased his influence and probably caused a revolution in the country. Besides that, she was probably afraid of what God would do to her if she touched his man. So her words were just an empty threat. She let Elijah escape to the desert because she didn't really intend to kill him. She just wanted to make him look like a coward in front of the nation. Or make him leave the area and thereby stop him from performing more miracles.

But Elijah didn't stop to evaluate the threat. Instead, he just ran away. *When we're depressed, we always exaggerate the negative.* Everything looks bad. If we're depressed, the whole world is going to pot. Realistically, Elijah was not the only person still faithful to God. There were still seven thousand prophets who hadn't succumbed to the pagan religion (v. 18). Elijah exaggerated the problem, and he sank lower than ever.

Another aspect of this is that we can fall into the trap of labeling ourselves. Instead of saying,

"I made a mistake," we say, "I'm a total failure." Instead of saying, "Oh, I accidentally tripped," we say, "I'm a klutz." Instead of saying, "I ate too much," we say, "I'm a pig." When we label ourselves with titles, it only reinforces our problems and makes things worse.

Applying God's Remedy

What was God's remedy for Elijah's depression? There are four things Elijah did to get rid of his doldrums that we can do to get rid of ours.

Take Care of Your Physical Needs

The first remedy is, *take care of your physical needs*. We read that Elijah stretched out under a tree and fell asleep. "All at once an angel touched him and said, 'Get up and eat.' He looked around, and there by his head was a cake of bread baked over hot coals, and a jar of water. He ate and drank and then lay down again" (1 Kings 19:5–6).

Then the angel came to him a second time and said, "Get up and eat, for the journey is too much for you" (v. 7). So he ate and drank and was strengthened by that food.

God's initial remedy for Elijah's depression was food, drink, and relaxation. Sometimes a good night's sleep does wonders for your attitude. When you are physically tired and mentally drained, you're prone to depression. Notice how tenderly God dealt with Elijah. God did not scold him by saying, "You coward! What are you doing here in the desert?" God didn't put him down or condemn him; all God did was give him food and rest. God physically restored Elijah. *That was the starting point.* If you are depressed, the first step toward recovery is to get in shape physically. Take care of your health needs. Maybe you need to watch your diet, or perhaps you need to get more sleep or begin an exercise program. Physical health has a profound influence on your moods.

Give Your Frustrations to God

The second remedy for your depression is to *give your frustrations to God.* After being restored through food and rest, Elijah traveled for forty days, and then went into a cave and spent the night there (vv. 8–9). In the morning the Lord asked him, "What are you doing here, Elijah?"

Elijah replied, "I have been very zealous for the LORD God Almighty. The Israelites have rejected your covenant, broken down your altars, and put your prophets to death with the sword. I am the only one left, and now they are trying to kill me too" (v. 10). Elijah poured out all his inner feelings. God allowed him to let off steam; he was not shocked by Elijah's complaints.

God says, in effect, "When you're uptight, let me hear your inner emotions. I already know what they are, and I'm not going to be shocked by them." He let Elijah vent his pent-up emotions without criticizing or condemning him. He listened. Often it is helpful to share your inner feelings with a Christian friend. It's a catharsis—a cleaning out, a venting, of all the things that have been pushed down inside you and are causing your depression.

And Elijah had pushed plenty down inside. Notice the six emotions he felt. First, he was *afraid* (v. 3). Then he felt *resentment* and had low self-esteem and felt *guilty*: "I'm fed up with it all, and I'm no better than my ancestors" (v. 4). He was *angry* that he had worked hard for nothing

(v. 10). He was *lonely* to the point of despair: "Now they are trying to kill me too" (v. 10). He was *worried*. When you combine fear, resentment, guilt, anger, loneliness, and worry, you are asking for depression!

So God just let him spill this all out. He said, "Elijah, what's frustrating you? What's eating you up?" Elijah poured it all out. When you are depressed, that's exactly what you need to do—tell it all to the Lord.

Get a Fresh Awareness of God

The third remedy for your depression is to *get a fresh awareness of God's presence in your life.* God told Elijah, "Go out and stand on the mountain in the presence of the LORD, for the LORD is about to pass by" (v. 11). Then a powerful wind tore the mountains apart and shattered the rocks. But the Lord wasn't in the wind. After the wind came an earthquake, but the Lord wasn't in the earthquake either. After the earthquake came a fire, but the Lord wasn't in the fire either. After the fire came a gentle whisper, and when Elijah heard this, he put his cloak over his face. He knew it was the Lord, so he went out and stood at the mouth of the cave (vv. 11–13).

God had put on an impressive show with the wind, the earthquake, and the fire, but he wasn't speaking to Elijah in any of those. What really got Elijah's attention was the still, small voice—the gentle whisper. Even today God usually speaks to us in stillness and quietness—not through some big dramatic demonstration of fire or power. God reminded Elijah that he was still right there beside him.

If you are depressed, take your Bible and go to a serene, quiet place like the ocean or a lake or a city park or a woods in the countryside. Sit down and read your Bible, and get alone with God. Just let God love you and speak to you. Let him meet your needs, and let yourself feel his presence. There is no greater antidepressant than communication and fellowship with God.

Gain a New Direction for Your Life

The fourth remedy for overcoming depression is to *let God give you a new direction for your life.* The Lord told Elijah, "Go back the way you came, and go to the Desert of Damascus. When you get there, here's what I want you to do" (see v. 15). Then God gave Elijah a new assignment—he put him back to work. The quickest way to defeat depression is to quit sitting around in self-pity. Get your eyes off yourself and start looking at the needs of other people. Get involved in their lives in a ministry where you are giving out and God is giving through you. If you are constantly looking at yourself, you will get discouraged. Jesus said, "Lose your life to find it" (see Matt. 16:25). Get involved in helping other people.

When we are depressed, we tend to think, "How could God ever use me? I'm such a failure. I keep making mistakes. I disappoint myself, so surely I must be disappointing God." *But you can never disappoint God*, because disappointment can only happen when somebody expects you to do something different from what you really do. The fact is that *God knows everything about you*. He knows how you will act in the future, so he's not disappointed when it happens. God knows that you are human, because he made you and he knows what makes you tick.

Let God give you a new purpose and a new direction. He's not through with you. You blew it? Big deal! If you let him, God will pick you up and help you start over. One mistake—or even a hundred—does not make you useless for life.

Jesus Christ wants to lift you out of your depression. He can help you; he can change you. You don't have to go through life being manipulated by your emotions. Your emotions are controlled by your thoughts, and you *can* control what you think about. You *can* choose to change your thoughts and thus indirectly control your emotions. Let God change those harmful misconceptions, such as:

"If somebody criticizes me, it means I'm worthless."

"I must be loved and accepted by *everybody* to be fulfilled in life."

"I cannot admit any area of weakness; I have to be perfect or else I'm a failure."

These are the kinds of misconceptions that cause depression. Jesus knew the importance of correct thinking when he said, "You will know the truth, and the truth will set you free" (John 8:32). The more you know Jesus, the freer you will be.

YOU CAN CHANGE

You *can* change. How do you start? By establishing a personal relationship with Christ. You become what the Bible calls "born again." This doesn't automatically cure all your depression, but without Christ in your life you have no power to change. With Christ in your life, you do have the power to change. He wants to be a vital part of your life, and if you give him control, he will help you. Once he is in your life, ask him to give you a new purpose and a new meaning in living.

You need something greater to live for than just yourself. People who live for themselves are guaranteed to get depressed. You need something greater that draws you out of yourself, and that is a vital relationship with Jesus Christ, God's strong Son.

PUTTING THOUGHTS INTO ACTION

1. Which of Elijah's mistakes are you most prone to experience in your life?
2. What is a specific way that you can begin working on the first remedy for depression — your physical well-being?

CHAPTER 4

HOW CAN I LIVE ABOVE AVERAGE?

G od never intended for you to live a medio-cre, average life. You are designed for excellence, and you were uniquely created. Instead of being one in a million, you are actually one in about six billion! Yet there's nobody else exactly like you; you are unique.

Everybody wants to be recognized. In fact, not only do you *want* to be recognized, but you *need* recognition, for the sake of your own emotional health and image. When my daughter Amy was very young, she would say to me, "Watch me, Daddy, watch me, Daddy!" She wanted to be recognized. She wanted to stand out from the crowd.

We as adults do the same thing, except we don't do it as blatantly. We do it with our cars and our clothing and our homes. All the time we're saying, "Watch me—everybody look at me!" Most of us have a need in our lives to be different, to be excellent, and to stand out from everybody else.

STANDING OUT IN THE CROWD

First Chronicles 4:9–10 tells us about a man named Jabez. The first nine chapters of this book consist of genealogies, with a listing of more than six hundred names. Right in the middle of all these names God singles out one man for special recognition, and his name is Jabez.

There are only two verses in the entire Bible on this man, yet he is given an honorable mention above six hundred other people. Why did God single out this man? What did he do that caused his name to be preserved for over four thousand years? What made him above average? The Bible says, "Jabez was *more honorable* than his brothers. His mother had named him Jabez, saying, 'I gave birth to him in pain'" (v. 9). (*Jabez* is the Hebrew word for "pain.")

Jabez prayed to God, "Oh, that you would bless me and enlarge my territory! Let your hand be with me, and keep me from harm so that I will be free from pain" (v. 10). And God granted his request.

There were three secrets to this man's life, revealing three principles that can make your life above average too.

Great Ambitions

The first secret is that Jabez had a great ambition. While all his friends were content with being average and mediocre, that wasn't enough for Jabez. He said, "I want God to bless me. I want something big. I want to do something significant with my life." He didn't want to be ordinary. He didn't want to be common. He wanted to expand and grow. He said, "God, bless me and enlarge my land." Jabez had a great ambition—and most of all, he deeply wanted God's blessing on his life. Many people today just drift through life. They have no goals, no master plan, no overall purpose, and no ambition. As a result, they never accomplish very much. They simply exist.

The first principle of living above average is that *you need a great ambition*. You need a dream. If you don't have a dream, you are drifting. When you stop dreaming, you lose direction. When you stop setting goals, you stop growing. You must have something that you're pushing toward: a goal of excellence. As long as your horizon is expanding, you will be an emotionally healthy human being. God made you for growth; he wants you to stretch and develop and dream. God has a purpose for your life, and your key to success is to discover that purpose and cooperate with it. God never intended for you to go through life with a halfhearted attitude, wondering what you're doing and where you're going. God wants you to have a great ambition in life. A life with no challenges and no goals can be summed up in one word: boring.

Three common misconceptions can keep us from having great ambitions. The first misconception is that *we confuse fear with humility*. We tend to say, "Oh, I could never do that," and we think we're being humble. But that is not humility. That is *fear*; that is *a lack of faith*. A truly humble person would say, "With God's help, I *can* do it. With God's blessing, I *will* do it. I may not be able to do it on my own, but with God's help I will do it." That's real humility.

Second, *we tend to confuse laziness with contentment*. It's true that Paul said, "I have learned to be content whatever the circumstances" (Phil. 4:11). But this doesn't mean that you shouldn't set any goals. Paul was not saying, "I've learned to not set any goals, and I don't have any ambitions or any future desires." He was saying that even though his goals may not have been reached yet, he had learned to enjoy every day to the fullest. He was saying, "I'm happy today even though I have dreams and ambitions that haven't been fulfilled yet."

If contentment were a valid excuse for laziness, who would ever feed the poor or do something about world hunger and equality and justice? How would anyone ever get an education? A third-grade kid would say, "I've learned to be content with the third grade," and he wouldn't go any farther. We must not confuse laziness with contentment.

Third, *we confuse small thinking with spirituality.* People have said to me, "I serve God in my little way." My reply is, "Well, why don't you start serving him in a bigger way? Let God use you more!"

Other people say, "Well, I'm just the way I am. That's the way God made me." But it is wrong to blame God for our lack of growth, because he has provided all the tools and ideas that we need in order to grow. Don't confuse small thinking with spirituality.

GROWING FAITH

The second principle for living above average is *you need a growing faith.* Not only did Jabez have a great ambition, but he also had a growing faith. He had a deep trust and belief in God. He had enough faith to pray and expect an answer. He was like the pioneer missionary William Carey, who said, "Attempt great things for God; expect great things from God."

The Bible gives us some interesting facts about Jabez. First, there's no mention of Jabez having any special ability or talent or gift. The Bible doesn't say that he was wealthy or educated. He was simply a common man with an uncommon faith. Don't worry about what else you *don't* have if you *do* have faith! God will give you the necessary power. God loves to use ordinary people who believe in him, who are willing to trust him, and see them succeed.

Jabez's faith caused him to believe that God would help him with his goals and his dreams. There is something more important than being talented, more important than ability or education—it's *faith*. It's believing that God will work through you. I've met many supertalented people who are sitting on the sidelines while ordinary people with faith are making the touchdowns. They believe God, so he uses them. Like Jabez, they are just ordinary people with extraordinary faith.

A second fact about Jabez is that he apparently had some type of handicap or disability. In the Hebrew language "Jabez" means "painful." How would you like to be named "Painful"? "Here comes Painful," or "There's old Painful over there." Jabez caused his mother so much grief during childbirth that she named him Painful. He may have been unwanted and unloved. His name constantly reminded him that even his birth caused grief in someone else's life. But Jabez was stronger than this handicap. His faith kept him going.

Regardless of his past painful experiences, Jabez had the faith to look ahead and attempt great things in the future.

What is your handicap? Is it physical? Is it spiritual? Is it an unhappy childhood? Is it a frustrating job or a broken marriage? Whatever it may be, God says, "Everything is possible for him who believes" (Mark 9:23).

GENUINE PRAYER

The third secret to Jabez's life was his *prayer life*. It was Jabez's simple prayer request that got him an honorable mention in the Bible. Lots of people pray without rising above average, and maybe you're one of them. Maybe you have hesitated to ask for things in prayer. Maybe you have felt your request was selfish. What kind of prayer does God answer? The life of Jabez illustrates three things we can ask God for and expect him to answer.

The first thing Jabez prayed for was *God's power in his life*. He asked for a power greater than his own to accomplish his dream. He prayed, "I want you to bless me. I want your power in my life."

It is important that Jabez's request was most specific: "God, this is what I want you to do: I want you to enlarge my coast; I want you to expand my territory; I want more real estate."

Do you pray about your goals? Do you ask God to help you wherever you're headed in your life? At first glance Jabez's prayer seems selfish, doesn't it? He prayed, "God, I want you to do all these things for me."

But evidently God approved of the prayer, because he answered it. Here is the point: *Ambition is neither good nor bad; it's just a basic drive in life.* Everyone has some ambition. It may be great or small, but everybody has some ambition in life. Maybe your ambition is just to get up in the morning, but you have to have some ambition to live in the world.

What makes ambition good or bad? One thing: the *motive* behind it. And Jabez's motives were genuine because God never honors an unworthy request. Consider this: *God dares you to ask for big requests.* What do you ask God for when you pray? God encourages you to ask for things: "You do not have, because you do not ask God" (James 4:2). The Lord said to Jeremiah, "Call to me and I will answer you and tell you great and unsearchable things you do not know" (Jer. 33:3). Paul says that God "is able to do immeasurably more than all we ask or imagine, according to his power that is at work within us" (Eph. 3:20). This means that you cannot out-ask God. You cannot out-dream God. If you could stretch your imagination to the greatest limits of what you think could possibly happen, God can go beyond even that.

He can go beyond *your* imagination. God says, "Trust me. Ask things. Find a great ambition, then get a growing faith, then bring them to me in genuine prayer."

What do you want God to do in your life? Heal a bad marriage situation? Ask him. Help you with a problem at work? Ask him. Help you fill a bigger niche in your church? Ask him. God is not some big policeman up in the sky waiting for you to make one wrong move so he can pounce on you; he *wants* to bless your life.

The second thing Jabez prayed for was *God's presence in his life*: "Let your hand be with me" (1 Chron. 4:10). Jabez realized that if he got more territory, it meant he would have more responsibility. He would have greater demands and more pressure, and he would really need God's help in his life. So he requested God to be with him. When you ask for God's presence in your life, you can be sure he will answer.

The third thing Jabez prayed for was *God's protection over his life*: "Keep me from harm so that I will be free from pain" (v. 10). Jabez asked God for his protection. Why did he do that? Because in those days, the more land you had, the more influence you had, and the better-known you were. And a bigger target.

It is still like that today: The more successful you are, the more critics you have. The more territory you own, the more enemies will attack you. The closer you grow to the Lord and the stronger you become as a Christian, the more the devil will harass you, because he doesn't want you to grow. But you can be sure, as Jabez was, that with God's protection you don't have to fear anyone or anything.

If you combine the three requests that Jabez prayed for, I guarantee that you will live above average. Do you want to break out of mediocrity? Do you want to see God work in your life? Do you want to see real answers to your prayers? Are you tired of drifting through life not knowing where you're going?

If you really want to live above average, if you want God's best for your life, then follow these three principles that Jabez used: Get a great ambition, a glimpse of what God wants to do in your life. Get a growing faith in God, a faith that enables you to expect the impossible. Establish a genuine prayer life, one that depends on God as you work toward your dream.

Putting Thoughts into Action

1. Which of the three "secrets" do you need to work on most right now? What specific steps will you take in that regard?
2. What is your biggest dream or goal, and what is the motive behind it?

CHAPTER 5

How Can I Have
Peace of Mind?

We live in a very tense, uptight world, which has been called the Age of Anxiety. We all face situations that make us irritable and tense and rob us of our peace of mind. Sometimes tension can be harmful to our health. Tension and stress are a major cause of heart attacks and high blood pressure. Every year more than 500 million dollars' worth of tranquilizers are prescribed to drop people into an emotional low gear.

Most of the tension we experience is basically the result of an unresolved conflict. If you have an argument with someone at work, you will be tense until you take the time to talk it out.

Unresolved issues also create tension in your life. If you have a major decision to make and you can't seem to decide what to do about it, it is upsetting and frustrating.

Yet there are some practical ways to gain peace of mind, and we learn them from a prominent figure in the Bible. Moses was a man who learned how to resolve the basic issues of life and as a result became a prime example of how to enjoy peace of mind.

THE MAN OF INNER PEACE

Moses is often considered the greatest man of faith in the Old Testament. In "God's Hall of Fame" of great men and women of faith (found in Hebrews 11), Moses gets more coverage than anyone else.

If anyone had a right to be uptight, it was Moses. From the very start, his life was filled with tension and conflict. The pharaoh of Egypt had proclaimed that every newborn Hebrew boy in the land of Egypt was to be killed. "By faith Moses' parents hid him for three months after he was born, because they saw that he was no ordinary child, and they were not afraid of the king's edict" (Heb. 11:23). Then, through unusual circumstances Moses was discovered and raised by the daughter of Pharaoh (Exod. 2:3–10). Yet,

> Moses, when he had grown up, refused to be known as the son of Pharaoh's daughter. He chose to be mistreated along with the people of God rather than to enjoy the pleasures of sin for a short time. He regarded disgrace for the sake of Christ as of greater value than the treasures of Egypt, because he was looking ahead to his reward. By faith he left Egypt, not fearing the king's anger (Heb. 11:24–27).

It was Moses' dream to lead two million Hebrews out of the land of Egypt, across the desert, and into a new country called Israel—the Promised Land. It was a great, God-inspired ambition. But nearly the entire time Moses was leading them, the people complained, argued, and fought. They just did not have enough faith to enter the Promised Land, so they spent forty years wandering around the wilderness. When all the original adults eventually died off, their children were allowed to enter. But by that time Moses had also died, so he was never able to see his dream fulfilled.

Moses had a right to be uptight, but the Bible says that he was a meek man. Now, "meek" does not mean "weak," even though that's often the first thought that comes to mind when people hear the word. Rather, meekness is an attitude of quiet confidence, of inner tranquility and peace of mind. Meekness keeps you from getting ruffled when things get hot. Meekness is the attitude that says, "When everybody's on my case, when things are uptight and I have every legitimate reason to get nervous and tense, I'm going to be cool. I'm not going to lose my temper." Only two people in the entire Bible were called meek: Jesus and Moses. So Moses is a prime example of how to enjoy peace of mind.

THE FOUR ISSUES OF LIFE

Why was Moses able to have this peace of mind? Why was he able to be at peace with himself? Because *Moses was a man of great principles.* Every decision he made was based on fundamental principles of life. He did not live by his feelings; instead, he based his life on God's principles for living. *God does not want us to build our lives around petty rules, but around great principles.* We see in Hebrews 11 that Moses came to grips with four fundamental issues of life that each of us can master. These arise from four basic questions.

First, Moses settled the question, "Who am I?" (v. 24). Next came the question, "What do I really want to be?" (v. 25). Then Moses addressed the question, "What is really important in life?" (v. 26). And the final question was, "How am I going to live?" (v. 27).

These are four bedrock issues that each one of us needs to come to grips with. In every case, Moses responded in the right way. He made the correct decision, and as a result we honor him today.

Know Who You Are

The first thing Moses dealt with is the issue of *identity*. He understood who he was. We need to understand the conflict here. Moses was actually a Hebrew, but Pharaoh's daughter raised him as an Egyptian, and everybody thought he was a bona fide Egyptian. But when he grew up, he somehow knew the truth, and he refused to be known as the son of Pharaoh's daughter. Years later, at about age forty, Moses was being groomed to be second in command in the kingdom, and he had to make a choice: "What am I going to do with my life? I am not whom most people think I am."

Moses had every comfort he could wish for in the palace, and he could have stayed there. But he had an identity crisis: "Who am I? Am I a Hebrew, or am I an Egyptian? Am I going to live with a bunch of Hebrew slaves, or am I going to stay here and live in luxury in the palace?" What would you have done? Moses made the right decision regarding this issue of identity, but it cost him the next eighty years of his life in the desert.

Every one of us must come to grips with our identity. We all have a deep want and need to accept who we are. To try to be somebody we are not is a quick way to get an ulcer, because the pressure is on. Moses recognized this tension, and he decided to quit pretending. He accepted his true identity.

It is a liberating experience when we relax and quit trying to be somebody we are not. The first foundation for peace of mind is, *Don't try to be someone you are not.* Relax and be yourself. God made you, and he loves you just the way you are, warts and all. You are very special to him.

You can pretend to be someone else, or you can accept God's plan and be who you were really meant to be in the first place. How would we remember Moses today if he had stayed in Pharaoh's court? Maybe as an Egyptian mummy in some museum, or maybe not at all. But he made the hard decision, and in the light of eternity it was the best one.

Among singer Anne Murray's biggest hits is the song "You Needed Me." It is about regaining hope and trust and inner strength. One line in the song sticks out: "You held me up and gave me dignity." God not only gives us an identity, but gives us *dignity* along with it. Every person Jesus dealt with in the New Testament—whether the woman caught in adultery or a leper or an outcast—was accepted and loved by him. Jesus said, "I know your name. You are a person."

When you quit trying to be somebody you are not, you can relax and let God work in your life.

ACCEPT YOUR RESPONSIBILITIES

The second issue Moses dealt with was the matter of *personal responsibility*. After he resolved the issue "Who am I?" he confronted the question "Who do I really want to be?" The Bible says that Moses chose to be mistreated with the rest of God's people rather than enjoy the sinful pleasures of Pharaoh's palace (Heb. 11:25). First he *refused* to be anyone but himself, and then he *chose* to go God's way. The principle is this: *You can always replace a negative with a positive.* You do not just stop doing something; you start doing something else. The Christian life is not a matter of negative rules and regulations; it is a matter of relationships—with God, with others, and with yourself. Someone has joked, "If all the Christian life consisted of was a list of don'ts, then everyone who is dead would qualify as a Christian!" But true Christianity isn't like that. God's way is a positive way.

Moses made his decision "when he had grown up" (v. 24). It is a mark of maturity when you settle the issue of personal responsibility. When Moses was a baby, it was okay for him to postpone the decision about who he was. But when he became an adult, he had to decide who he was. He had to make a choice, assume responsibility for his own life, and move ahead.

The need for personal responsibility is an unpopular truth in our society today. We live in a culture that loves to blame others and not accept personal responsibility. Who was responsible for the 1973 oil crisis? The Americans blamed the Arabs, the Arabs blamed the oil companies, the oil companies blamed the U.S. government, and the government blamed the ecologists. Nobody wanted to accept any blame.

All of us love to *give* blame, but we all hate to *be* blamed. It is easy to blame others for your condition: "I'd be more committed to Christ if my family were Christians." "I would really go God's way if my boyfriend or girlfriend or mother or father or husband or wife would get going." "I would be a better person today if I had better parents." Moses didn't blame anyone else: he assumed the responsibility for his own life.

It is true, of course, that there are many things in life over which you have no control. You had no control over who your parents were. You had no control over where you were born. You had no control over the genes that went into your makeup. But there is one thing you have absolute control over, and that is *your response* toward life. You can choose to respond toward life in a negative, critical manner, or you can choose to respond toward life in a positive manner of faith.

But what about those times when other people create problems for you? True, you can't control them. But you can choose how you respond to them. A survivor of a German concentration camp said the only thing he learned was that, though he could not control what happened to him, he *could* control how he responded to it. Nobody can take away your attitude unless you give it away. When you assume responsibility for your own attitude, then you can start enjoying true peace of mind.

You cannot choose all the circumstances that come into your life, but you *can* choose whether those things will make you a bitter person or a better person. It is your responsibility. *No one can ruin your life except you!* The devil can't, because he doesn't have enough power. God won't, because he loves you. Only *you* can ruin your own life.

Decide Your Priorities

There is a third issue that Moses faced. "He chose to be mistreated along with the people of God rather than to enjoy the pleasures of sin for a short time" (Heb. 11:25). He regarded this sacrifice for the sake of Christ as of greater value than the treasures of Egypt. Moses faced the issue of *priorities*. He knew what was really important in life.

From the human standpoint, young Moses had everything. Much of the world's wealth during that time was stored in Egypt. Moses had what most people spend their entire lives trying to get: power, pleasure, and possessions.

Yet God asked Moses to do something that was more important—and he did it. It was a matter of priority in his life. Because Moses was considered the son of Pharaoh's daughter and was in a position of great power, he could have rationalized,

"The slave situation is bad, so I'll just stay in the system and work for reform."

But God didn't say that. He told Moses, "Get out there and get moving!"

Most people want to be liked in their community, but there is one problem with popularity: it never lasts. You can be Big Man on Campus for a while, but when you return a few years after graduation, you will find that nobody considers you anybody special. Popularity just does not last.

Then there is pleasure. Is pleasure wrong? No, it isn't wrong to have pleasure unless it is your god. We live in a pleasure-obsessed society: "You only go around once in life, so you had better do it with gusto." "Do your own thing." "If it feels good, do it." But the problem is that pleasure, like popularity, does not last. Moses rejected temporary pleasures because he had his values right; he had his vision on something higher.

There is nothing inherently wrong with having money. Some of the greatest saints of the Bible were extremely wealthy, including Job, Abraham, and David. But the Bible says that "a man's life does not consist in the abundance of his possessions" (Luke 12:15). Ultimately, wealth does not bring happiness. Ask the people who have it. How much money does it take to be happy? Usually just a little bit more. *Money is to be used, not loved.* God wants us to use things and love people. But if we love things, we will use people. Moses had his priorities right; he rejected material things because there was something more important in his life.

Face Your Difficulties

The final issue Moses settled was the matter of *perseverance.* We could almost sum up Moses' life in two words: "he endured" (Heb. 11:27 KJV). It is a fact of life that there is no gain without pain, no advancement without adversity, no progress without problems. On the issue of endurance, learn how to relate to difficulties.

Moses made a success of his life because he endured. The key to his peace of mind was that he knew difficulties come into every life, and he knew how to respond to them correctly and move on. As Christians we should never let problems destroy us; we should let problems draw us closer to God. Someone has said that Christians should never let problems get them down, except down on their knees. God allows these situations in our lives for specific reasons.

Without persistence we won't go far in life. Peace of mind comes when we accept responsibility for our choices, choose God's priorities, and then confidently persevere.

Moses was a man who learned how to resolve the basic issues of life, and as a result became a prime example of how to enjoy peace of mind. Because he made the right decisions and settled what is important in life, he was able to live with himself and assume a tremendous responsibility, yet remain calm under pressure.

Whether you are a teenager, a senior citizen, or something in between, you eventually have to deal with these fundamental issues. If you can learn to settle these issues in your mind, you will know what it means to have real peace of mind. You will learn how to be calm in a crisis, how to be strong under stress, and how to be at peace under pressure. And you can learn from experience how to stay that way.

Putting Thoughts into Action

1. Who are you? If you were talking to God, what words would you use to describe your true identity?

2. What is one thing that you feel should have greater priority in your life, and what is one immediate step you can take toward that end?

CHAPTER 6

How Can I Handle Discouragement?

If you were asked to name the world's deadliest disease, what would be your answer? Cancer? Polio? MS? AIDS? You probably wouldn't say *discouragement*. You might not even think of discouragement as a deadly disease, but it is. And it is more common than any of those others.

Why is discouragement such a dreaded disease? First, because it's universal. All of us get discouraged. I do, you do, we all do. Discouragement is common. Yes, even Christians get discouraged. Second, because it's recurring. You can get discouragement a number of times. It's not just a one-time thing. Third, because it's highly contagious.

Other people can get discouraged because *you're* discouraged.

NOW THE GOOD NEWS

The good news is that discouragement is curable. A story from the life of Nehemiah illustrates four causes and three cures for discouragement. You may recall that the man Nehemiah was a leader of the Jewish group that had returned to Israel from Babylon to rebuild the wall around Jerusalem. When they first started on the wall, they had a lot of fervor and zeal and were very excited about the project. But after working for a while, they became discouraged.

Chapter 4 of the book of Nehemiah has the people starting out on a high note. "So we rebuilt the wall till all of it reached half its height, for the people worked with all their heart" (v. 6). But as the story continues, the mood changes: "Meanwhile, the people in Judah said, 'The strength of the laborers is giving out, and there is so much rubble that we cannot rebuild the wall.' Also our enemies said, 'Before they know it or see us, we will be right there among them and will kill them and put an end to the work.' Then the Jews who live near them came and told us ten times over, 'Wherever you turn, they will attack us'" (vv. 10–12).

We have probably had this mood more often than we want to remember. You may be discouraged right now. This story shows why people become discouraged and how they can overcome that discouragement. It tells us what to do when we feel like giving up.

Why We Become Discouraged

Just Plain Tired

Why do people get discouraged? The first reason is *fatigue*. The people in Judah said, "The strength of the laborers is giving out." In other words, they had worked themselves to exhaustion. They were just plain worn out—physically, mentally, and emotionally drained.

Sometimes people come to me for counseling who are feeling discouraged and incorrectly think it is a spiritual problem. They say, "Maybe I just need to recommit my life to the Lord." But their real problem is that they are just burned out. They need some rest, relaxation, and renewal. So I tell them, "You don't need to recommit your life—you just need some rest." Sometimes the most spiritual thing you can do is just go to bed and relax, or take an affordable two-week vacation.

When do fatigue and discouragement occur? Look at verse 6: "So we rebuilt the wall till all of it reached half its height." Do you know when you're apt to get discouraged the most? When you're halfway through a project. Everybody works hard at first. These people "worked with all their heart" (v. 6). Why? Because of the newness of the project. It was exciting and novel at first, but after a while the newness wore off and the work got boring. Life settled down into a rut, then a routine, then a ritual.

Have you ever painted a room? You get halfway through it and then look around and say, "Man, I'm getting tired, and I'm just half finished. Not only that, but after I'm finished, I've got to clean everything up."

I did a fatiguing thing not long ago: I tried to reorganize my filing cabinets. Do you know what it means to clean out your filing cabinets? It means that you take all the things out of your file, then put them in different piles all over the floor; then you get discouraged and put everything back the way it was!

Have you ever started to hike up a mountain trail and thought, "It'll only take me two hours to get to the top"? But when you are only halfway up the trail, you have already spent three hours hiking! So you think, "Shall I keep going? I've got to go that far back down again too!" Suddenly you start thinking, "Maybe it's God's will that I go back down." But that can be just a cop-out, an excuse to give up. Fatigue is the number one cause of discouragement, and it often happens right about the midpoint. That is why so many people leave so many things unfinished and undone.

Trashed by Frustration

But there is a second factor in a person's becoming discouraged. The Israelites said, "There is so much rubble that we cannot rebuild the wall" (v. 10). That's *frustration*. They were disheartened and frustrated over what seemed to be an impossible situation. What's rubble? They were building a new wall, but old, broken rocks were everywhere, along with dirt and dried-out mortar. When they looked at the rubble and the debris, they became discouraged. They lost sight of their goal because there was so much junk in their lives that they didn't know how to get to the real business of living.

Whenever you do a project, some waste is going to accumulate, and it can get to be pretty frustrating. Have you ever expanded a room or constructed a building? All of a sudden you notice piles of plaster all over the place. Or you paint a room, and there's too much paint in places where it shouldn't be—on the floor or on the window frames. The trash just seems to multiply. You cannot avoid rubbish in life, but you *can* learn to recognize it and you *can* learn what to do with it so you do not give up on your original plan.

What is the rubbish in your life? It is the trivial things that waste your time and consume your energy and keep you from becoming all you want to be. It is the things that keep you from doing what is really most important in life, such as nurturing your spouse and children, or being active in your areas of giftedness at church. The rubbish in your life is those things that get in your way, the interruptions that keep you from accomplishing your goals. These are the things we need to clean away in our lives. We need to take out the trash.

Stalled by Failure

A third reason why people become discouraged is also reflected in the Israelites' complaint. They said, "We cannot rebuild the wall" (v. 10). Do you know what they were saying? "We're too tired. It's not possible. It's foolish to try. We give up." The problem here is *failure*. The people were unable to finish their task as quickly as they had originally planned, and as a result their confidence plummeted. They lost heart and got discouraged. They said, "We can't do it, so we're just going to give up."

How do you handle failure in your life? Do you have a pity party? Do you say, "Oh, poor me! I can't get this job done"? Do you start complaining? "It's impossible. It can't be done. I was a fool to even try. It's stupid."

Or do you blame other people? "Everybody else let me down. They didn't do their part of the job." There is a difference between winners and losers, and it is that the winners always see failure as being only a temporary setback.

Stopped by Fear

There is a fourth reason why people get discouraged. Nehemiah's people put it this way: "Our enemies said, 'Before they know it or see us, we will be right there among them and will kill them and put an end to the work'" (v. 11). There were people in the land of Israel who did not want the wall to be rebuilt; they were the enemies of the Jews. A wall around the city represented safety and defense, so these enemies did not want the wall to be finished. So first they criticized the Jews, then they ridiculed them, and finally they threatened them: "We're going to kill you if you keep on building the wall." So the wall-builders became discouraged. Why? Because of the fourth cause of discouragement: *fear.*

Notice who became discouraged. It was "the Jews who lived near" the enemy (v. 12). Then they discouraged others by saying, "Wherever you turn, they will attack us." When you hang around a negative person long enough, you know what happens. You pick up his negativism too. If you hear someone repeatedly say, "It can't be done," you will start believing her.

Do you have fears that are making you discouraged right now—fears that are preventing you from developing and growing? Do you fear criticism or embarrassment? Are you afraid to take the big step and get the new job? Maybe it's a fear that you are not capable for the task. Maybe it's a fear that you can't hold up under the pressure. Maybe it's a fear that you have to be perfect. *Fear always discourages you.*

How can you tell if your discouragement is being caused by fear? You have a deep, intense desire to run. You have an intense desire to escape from life's demands and pressures. The natural reaction of fear is always to run. In life there are only three ways you can move—*against* something in anger, *away from* it in fear, or *with* it in love.

How to Overcome Discouragement

What is the antidote to this terrible disease of discouragement? Notice what Nehemiah did as a wise leader and a man of God. He knew what it was that discouraged people, so he took the appropriate actions to correct the problem. There are three principles to help you when you feel like giving up, and they are *reorganize*, *remember*, and *resist*.

Find a Better Way

Nehemiah used the *reorganize* principle: "Therefore I stationed some of the people behind the lowest points of the wall at the exposed places, posting them by families, with their swords, spears and bows" (v. 13). Nehemiah said in effect, "We're going to get this thing really organized. We're going to get a new system here. You people go over there, and you other people stand here, and we'll get this problem solved."

The first principle in conquering discouragement is this: *Reorganize your life*. When you get discouraged, *don't give up on your goals*. Instead, *devise a new approach*. When you are disheartened, it doesn't necessarily mean that you're doing the wrong thing; you can be doing the right thing in the wrong way. Was it wrong for these Jews to be building the wall? Absolutely not; it was the right thing. But they were going about it in the wrong way, and as a result they became discouraged.

Do you have a problem? Reorganize your life. A problem in your marriage? Don't give up on it. Try a new attitude. A problem in your business? Don't give up on it. Try a new approach. A problem in your Christian living? Don't give up on it. Try a new prayer. A problem with your health? Try a new doctor. *Don't give up. Keep on keeping on.*

Some of you are discouraged because you are under tremendous pressure; your workload is unbelievable. God's message to you is *reorganize.* Reorganize your time, reorganize your schedule, and refocus on your goal. Clear out the clutter and rubble and trivia—the things that are wasting your time. Then reorganize so you work better, faster, more efficiently toward your main goal.

I was reminded at a seminar of the 80/20 principle: About 80 percent of our time is usually spent on the 20 percent of our activities that are not productive. As a result we are frustrated. What we need to do instead is spend 80 percent of our time on the 20 percent of our job that produces the most results. Business managers call this ROI time — "Return on Investment" time. In other words, use the maximum time on those few things that produce the greatest results or have the greatest consequences.

Notice that Nehemiah focused on priorities. When he reorganized, he posted the people by families. Why? Because he knew that anyone who is discouraged needs a support group. We need other people for support, and families are a natural group. When one person in a family gets discouraged, other members will lift him up. We need fellow Christians who support each other and encourage one another. When I get down, you lift me up, and when you get down, I lift you up. That's a support group.

Solomon said,

"Two are better than one,
        because they have a good return
        for their work:
If one falls down,
        his friend can help him up.
But pity the man who falls
        and has no one to help him up!

Also, if two lie down together, they will keep
warm.
But how can one keep warm alone?
Though one may be overpowered,
two can defend themselves.
A cord of three strands is not quickly broken"
(Eccl. 4:9–12).

What is Solomon saying? That it is important
to have other people in our lives to help us and
encourage us.

Remember Your Leader

A second way to overcome discouragement is to
remember the Lord. Notice what Nehemiah said:
"After I looked things over, I stood up and said
to the nobles, the officials and the rest of the
people, 'Don't be afraid of them. *Remember the
Lord*, who is great and awesome'" (Neh. 4:14).
What does it mean to "remember the Lord"? It
means to recommit yourself to him. It means to
rededicate yourself to him. It means to draw on
his spiritual power.

What specifically should you remember? Three
things: first, remember God's goodness to you in

the past. When you start thinking about all the good things that God has already done in your life, your spirit will be lifted and your anxiety eased. Second, remember God's closeness in the present. What is he doing in your life right now? He is with you whether or not you feel his nearness, because he said, "Never will I leave you; never will I forsake you" (Heb. 13:5). You may not be calling on God, but he is still there. Third, remember God's power for the future. He will give you strength for your needs. When you get discouraged, get your mind off your circumstances and focus on the Lord, because circumstances depress and discourage.

Keep in mind that your thoughts determine your feelings. If you feel discouraged, it is because you are thinking discouraging thoughts. If you want to feel *encouraged* instead, start thinking encouraging thoughts. Choose some uplifting Bible verses to memorize:

> "I can do everything through him who gives me strength" (Phil. 4:13).

Nothing "in all creation will be able to separate us from the love of God" (Rom. 8:39).

"If God is for us, who can be against us?" (Rom. 8:31).

"Everything is possible for him who believes" (Mark 9:23).

Fight the Gloomy Outlook

How else do you fight discouragement? By resisting it. Notice what Nehemiah says: "Fight for your brothers, your sons and your daughters, your wives and your homes" (Neh. 4:14). What is Nehemiah saying? He is telling us not to yield to discouragement without a fight. *Resist discouragement.* Fight it. Don't give in to it, but resist it.

The Bible teaches that Christians are in a spiritual warfare—a battle. We are in a supernatural conflict, a combat with negative forces. The Bible says that the devil is the accuser of Christians; he loves to get us down. That is his number one tool, because he knows that a discouraged Christian has limited potential. He knows that when we are down, our effectiveness is neutralized. So he does everything he can to discourage us. The book of James says, "Resist the devil" (4:7). Resist him and his negative thoughts—all the discouragement he tries to bring into your life.

You do not have to be discouraged in life. It is your choice. You may choose to give in, but great people simply refuse to be discouraged. They don't know how to quit. They never give up even when they are fatigued and frustrated and have failed and are fearful. Great people are ordinary people with extraordinary amounts of persistence. They just hang in there and never give up.

Putting Thoughts into Action

1. Which of the four causes of discouragement affects you most at this time?
2. What do you like to "remember" most about God when you are discouraged, and how does that help you?

CHAPTER 7

HOW CAN I OVERCOME
MY PROBLEMS?

The well-known story of Jehoshaphat describes one of the greatest epic battles in the history of Israel. Jehoshaphat, the king of Israel, received word from a friend that the combined armies of three enemy nations were on their way to fight him and conquer him. The chronicler tells us that these three nations were the Moabites, the Ammonites, and the Meunites (2 Chron. 20:1), and all were nearby—just beyond the Jordan River or the Dead Sea. The odds were definitely not in Jehoshaphat's favor.

This story is relevant to each of us because we all face battles each day: financial, spiritual, marital, vocational, relational—all kinds of battles in our daily lives. God put the story of Jehoshaphat in the Bible in order to illustrate certain vital spiritual principles in winning the battles of life.

IDENTIFY THE ENEMY

Second Chronicles 20:1 shows us the first principle in overcoming the battles of life: *identify the enemy.* This seems like a rather obvious principle, but actually it is not. Many people simply do not know who their enemy is. We often think the enemy is a person who is trying to take something from us—our job, our spouse, our money—but very often the enemy is our own attitude. It is not so much the *situation* that gets us down but *our response to the situation.* Before we can start winning our personal battles, we have to accurately and honestly identify the enemy.

Notice how Jehoshaphat reacted when he heard that these three nations were coming against him: he was alarmed (v. 3). This is a typical reaction for everyone. When we see a big problem, we panic and become unsure of what is going to happen. "What's going to happen to me? I'm starting to get afraid!" This is a natural reaction to problems, and fear is not bad unless we deal with it in the wrong way. We can use fear to motivate ourselves to conquer the problem. But if we become discouraged and give up, or get angry with God and ask, "Why me?" then fear defeats us.

Admit Your Inadequacy

Jehoshaphat was afraid because he was facing what seemed to be a hopeless situation. He cried out to the Lord, "We have no power to face this vast army that is attacking us. We do not know what to do" (2 Chron. 20:12). This illustrates the second principle in winning the battles of life: *Admit your inadequacy.* There is only one kind of person God doesn't help: someone who doesn't think he needs help. When you admit your inadequacy and ask for help, God can work on it.

After Jehoshaphat admitted that he and his counselors didn't know what to do, he prayed, "But our eyes are upon you" (v. 12). We need to get our eyes focused on the Lord. Too often we have our eyes on everything except the one who can solve our problems. Circumstances are like a mattress: If we're on top, we rest easy, but if we're underneath, we might suffocate. If we keep our eyes on the Lord, we will win out over our circumstances.

We can't live out the Christian life on our own, because we have a power shortage. We need the power that comes from God. We live the Christian life "not by might nor by power, but by [God's] Spirit" (Zech. 4:6). We need to let God's Spirit live through us.

TAKE IT TO THE LORD

So in the midst of this crisis, what did Jehoshaphat do? He proclaimed a fast and had all the people come together to seek out the Lord (2 Chron. 20:3–4). People came from every town in Judah to ask God for help. The third principle in winning the battles of life is to *take your problems to the Lord*.

This means praying. Unfortunately, prayer is often the last thing we try, because we want to be able to work things out on our own.

A deacon came to his pastor one day and said, "Pastor, we've really got a problem. Nothing's happening, and we can't solve the problem."

The pastor said, "Well, I guess all we can do is pray about it."

The deacon replied, "Pastor, has it come to that?"

Prayer ought to be the *first* weapon we use—not the last—whenever we face the battles of life. It is important to remember that Jesus fought the biggest battles in life, and he also prayed the most.

Jehoshaphat prayed, in effect, "God, I know you have helped me in the past. I know you can help me in the future. So please help me *now*."

RELAX IN FAITH

Notice how God responded to Jehoshaphat's prayer: "Do not be afraid or discouraged because of this vast army. For the battle is not yours, but God's" (v. 15). The fourth principle in overcoming life's battles is to *relax in faith*. Many Christians today are totally worn out because they are trying to fight God's battles in their own strength. If we try to fight God's battles in our own power, we are sure to be defeated.

When we first become Christians, we may not really understand what we have gotten ourselves into. In our enthusiasm we may think we are ready to go out and bring in God's kingdom single-handedly. We are eager to win the world for him. Then we work very hard and reality sets in, and eventually we come crawling back on our hands and knees, feeling remorseful and disappointed that we have let God down.

But God replies, "No, you didn't let me down, because you weren't holding me up." *We don't hold up God; he holds us up. We don't have God in our hands; he has us in his hands.* God is trying to tell us, "Relax in faith and let me work through you."

There was a time in my life as a Christian when I had been working diligently for the Lord, but doing everything under my own power. And I was so tired. Finally I couldn't take it anymore. I said, "Lord, this stinks! I don't like it. I'm tired. I'm sick and tired. In fact, I'm sick and tired of being sick and tired."

Then I said, "God, I give up."

At that moment I heard this voice saying, "Great! Now *I* can start working, because as long as you're out there trying to make your own plans and do it on your own, you're just going to mess things up. Relax—let me work through you."

The apostle Paul said, "As you *received* Christ Jesus as Lord, *continue to live in him*" (Col. 2:6). In other words, as you look at the way you *became* a believer, be sure to *live* the Christian life the same way. It's a choice. The Bible says that salvation is "not by works, so that no one can boast" (Eph. 2:9). You didn't become a Christian by working really hard at being good, by promising to be perfect, by doing your very best. You did it by simply saying to God, "Lord, I relax; I let you live in my life." We should *continue* as Christians in the same way and let God manage things. Victory in life is a gift from God: "Thanks be to God! He gives us the victory!" (1 Cor. 15:57).

Twice in this passage (2 Chron. 20:15, 17) God instructed Jehoshaphat not to be afraid. The king thought he had every reason in the world to fear—after all, it was three-to-one odds against him. But God said, "Do not be afraid." Why not?

Because God promised to fight the battle for us and with us.

Has God ever lost a battle? No! Not ever. So you know who is going to win in the end. It's like reading the last chapter of a novel so you can know it is going to end all right, and then going back and relaxing through the story. Your problems shrink in size when you turn them over to the Lord.

Notice what else God said to Jehoshaphat: "You will not have to fight this battle. Take up your positions; *stand firm*" (v. 17). What does it mean to stand firm when you have a problem, when you are facing a battle, when you are having a life crisis? It is a mental attitude of quiet confidence that says, "I'm going to trust God."

This is something I am slowly learning: *It is never God's will for me to run from a difficult situation*. If I do run, the situation will only follow and catch up with me a little farther down the line. It may not look the same, but it will *be* the same. Why? Because God wants to teach me that he is sufficient for any problem. If we don't learn this today, we may learn it next week. If we don't learn it next week, we may learn it next year—eventually we will learn it. The sooner the better. We can save ourselves problems by standing firm and waiting on God in quiet confidence.

So what do we stand firm on? Jehoshaphat says that we are to have faith in the Lord our God, and we will be upheld; to have faith in his prophets, and we will be successful. First, we need to stand firm on the character of God. God is faithful, and we can depend on him; he will never let us down. Second, we need to stand firm on the writings that God has given through his prophets—in other words, the truth of the Bible. The Bible is God's Word, and we need to rely in quiet confidence on his written promises.

THANK GOD IN ADVANCE

The fifth principle in conquering life's battles is to *thank God in advance for giving you the victory.* The story of Jehoshaphat is fascinating, because after he consulted the people, he appointed men to sing to the Lord, to praise God for his splendor and holiness as they went out at the head of the army (v. 21).

Now get the picture: Imagine you are standing on a mountaintop and looking across a valley toward a mountain on the other side. A big battle is about to take place down below. On one mountain are the three enemy nations, just waiting to devastate the Israelites. The Israelites are on your mountain, and their leader, Jehoshaphat, tells them, "Here's God's battle plan. All of those who sing in the choir, I want you out front." So the army goes marching to battle with the choir out in front, singing praises to God.

Did God's plan work? Yes. The three enemy armies got confused and ended up killing each other! All God's people had to do was to divide up the plunder. Why did God do it this way? As a visual object lesson to teach us to praise him in faith even before the victory takes place.

A boy named James was not a believer, and in fact was anti-Christian. One day his mother bought him a Bible, laid it on his desk, and said, "Here, son, is your new Bible."

James replied, "What's this for?"

His mother answered, "You don't know it yet, but you're about to become a Christian."

James responded, "No I'm not. I'm going to play football and go to hell."

His mother stood up in church that night and said, "My son is about to become a Christian. He doesn't know it yet, but I'm thanking God in advance."

So James's friends began to walk up to him on the street and say, "I heard you became a Christian."

"No, it's just my crazy mother. I'm going to play football and go to hell."

But his mother told her pastor, "I want you to save twenty minutes on Saturday night for my son to give his testimony."

The Friday night before that Saturday, James was playing football when he suddenly felt God's presence right on the playing field. He got down on his knees and prayed right in front of everybody: "God, I really need you in my life. If you can make a difference, come in and change me. Save me, whatever it takes. Make me born again."

James ran off the field in his uniform, down the street, and up the stairs into his house. He hugged his mother and proclaimed, "Mom, I just became a Christian!"

She replied, "Of course! I've been telling you that for three weeks!"

This is a true story of thanking God in advance. The lesson is that *there is power in thankfulness.* Each one of us can say, "Lord, I know I have problems, but I thank you in advance because there is no situation that you can't take care of." That's true faith—thanking God in advance.

Putting Thoughts into Action

1. What is one attitude you need to change in confronting the problems you are facing right now?

2. What is one situation that you can thank God in advance for resolving?

CHAPTER 8

HOW CAN I BE CONFIDENT IN A CRISIS?

THE STORMS OF LIFE

The Bible teaches us that there are three kinds of storms in life: storms that we bring on ourselves (like Samson and his self-induced troubles), storms that God causes (like the one that Jesus stilled on Lake Galilee), and storms that other people cause (as when Paul and Silas were thrown into prison). When you are the innocent party in a crisis, that last kind of storm is especially hard to take.

So how do we deal with these crises? How do we stay calm and maintain our confidence and courage, regardless of what happens?

God put the apostle Paul, as a prisoner, on board a ship headed from Palestine to Rome. (Actually, Paul had a great desire to go to Rome and preach, but he hadn't planned on this being the means of getting there.) After the ship ventured through the Mediterranean Sea and docked at the island of Crete, God told Paul to advise the crew not to leave the harbor because there was going to be a great storm. But the sailors were impatient to get to a better harbor, so they ignored what God had told them through Paul (Acts 27:9–12).

Impatience often gets us into trouble. When we allow ourselves to become impatient, we find ourselves faced with a storm. I have spoken with many crisis-ridden people who were impatient: impatient to get married, impatient to get a new job, or impatient to move to the other side of town. They didn't take time to check things out with God, and they sailed right off into the awaiting storms.

Paul told the sailors, "Men, I can see that our voyage is going to be disastrous and bring great loss to ship and cargo, and to our own lives also"

(v. 10). But they sailed into the storm anyway. Why? Because they were following human nature. There are three common reasons why people get themselves in a mess. And these reasons hold true, whether the mess happened about two thousand years ago in the book of Acts or happens today, because human nature has not changed!

How We Get into a Crisis

Wrong Guidance from the Experts

The centurion who had charge over Paul ignored his plea and instead followed the advice given by both the captain and the owner of the ship. They left the harbor. This points up the first reason we get ourselves into a mess: *we listen to the wrong experts.*

The world is full of people with crazy ideas, and it seems as if every week someone is proposing a new therapy or a new cult. One person will say, "The key to life is to eat bananas and yogurt." Someone else will say, "No, the key to life is to put yourself in some strange position and go 'ommm.'" A third person will say, "No, the key to life is to buy our seminar tapes." It seems that everybody has a way; everybody has an expert opinion. But the fact is that experts are often wrong. Some people go around asking experts what they think until they find a person who agrees with them, just to substantiate their own biases. When you start asking the wrong experts, you are going to get yourself into a mess—or a storm. The only truly reliable expert is God.

Wrong Guidance from a Vote

Because the harbor where they were docked was unsuitable in winter, the majority of the crew decided that the ship should sail on. They hoped to reach Phoenix and its safe harbor on the other side of Crete (v. 12). The second reason we get ourselves in trouble is that *we take a vote*. The fact is that the majority can be wrong. Do you remember what happened when Moses first started to lead the children of Israel toward the Promised Land? The majority wanted to return to Egypt, but they were wrong. We can get ourselves into a real mess by following the prevailing opinion, the most popular ideas. If we listen to God, we will go in the right direction.

Wrong Guidance from Circumstances

The story continues: "When a gentle south wind began to blow, they [the ship's crew] thought they had obtained what they wanted; so they weighed anchor and sailed along the shore of Crete" (v. 13). It proved to be a bad decision. Why else do we get ourselves into trouble? Because *we rely on circumstances*. Notice that the Bible says there was a gentle south wind. What could be better for a nice, gentle Mediterranean cruise? The sailors thought they had gotten their wish because the circumstances looked favorable. But it is foolish and unwise to ignore what God says, even if circumstances tend to contradict it. Things may look good right now, but you may be sailing right into a storm.

I have heard people say, "Well, this decision must be okay because I feel so good about it." A popular song from the 1970s says, "It can't be wrong when it feels so right." As we saw in chapter 3, the fact is that feelings often lie. If God says, "Wait in the harbor," you had better wait in the harbor, because the devil can arrange undesirable circumstances if you put out to sea.

As I talk with people in counseling, I hear over and over again that they thought they had obtained what they wanted but then went sailing right into a storm, just as the sailors in the book of Acts did. They found themselves caught in "a wind of hurricane force, called the 'northeaster'" (v. 14). The ship—like so many couples I counsel—became caught in the storm and could not head into the wind.

WHAT NOT TO DO IN A CRISIS

Don't Drift

When we are caught in a crisis, we typically react in three ways—the same three ways the sailors did. Their reactions were typical of people under pressure. Because the sailors couldn't head into the wind, "we gave way to it and were driven along" (v. 15). Later, "they lowered the sea anchor and let the ship be driven along" (v. 17). The first thing that storms tend to do is to cause us to drift. We let go of our goals. We forget where we are headed. *We forget our values and start drifting.*

Because they were not equipped with compasses and the stars were completely obscured by the storm, the sailors were in total darkness. When you are in a dark situation in which you can't see the stars and don't have a compass, what do you do? You drift. The waves beat you back and forth, and you are led wherever they take you. Your problems batter you back and forth. These strong currents in your life can make you feel like asking, "What's the use? Why fight it?" And we just go with the flow.

Don't Discard

Things didn't get any better on the apostle Paul's voyage to Rome. "We took such a violent battering from the storm that the next day they began to throw the cargo overboard. On the third day they threw the ship's tackle overboard with their own hands" (vv. 18 – 19). When a crisis emerges for us, first we start drifting, and then *we start discarding things from our lives*. With the sailors it was first the cargo, then the ship's tackle, eventually their food (v. 38), and finally themselves (vv. 43 – 44)! They all jumped overboard and started swimming to shore.

Often, when we find ourselves in a crisis of life, we are tempted to throw out the very things that are important to us, the values that we have hung onto in better times. We have a tendency to throw things out, because we are under pressure and want to get rid of it all. We become impulsive. We give up on our dreams. We run out on relationships. We throw away values that we learned as children.

Don't Despair

The third thing that the sailors did was to give up hope. "When neither sun nor stars appeared for many days and the storm continued raging, we finally gave up all hope of being saved" (v. 20). In an extreme crisis *we eventually get to the point of despair and give up all hope.* The last thing we throw out when we have a problem is hope, and when we have thrown that away, we have "had it."

The sailors spent fourteen days in total darkness in a little ship in the middle of the Mediterranean Sea. They were bashed back and forth by the storm until they threw out everything and gave up all hope. Perhaps you feel like that right now. Have you been going through a problem the past week or past month or past year that has been batting you back and forth? Have you come to the point where you have thrown things out, and now you have come to the point of despair? Remember the sailors: they gave up hope because they had forgotten that *God is in control*. They forgot that God had a plan. They forgot that God can inject hope into an absolutely hopeless situation.

Paul's Reaction to the Crisis

The amazing part of this story is Paul's reaction. It is a 180-degree turnaround from the way the sailors responded to this crisis. The sailors were in despair; they said the situation was hopeless. They were discouraged and depressed and tossed everything overboard to try to keep the ship afloat.

But Paul provides a different model for us. He was calm and confident. He had courage in the crisis. Absolutely nothing fazed him.

The sailors' reactions were the natural responses that we tend to have in a crisis, but they do not have to be our reactions. One test of our Christianity is how we handle a crisis. It is easier to live like a Christian when things are going great, when all our prayers are being answered, when we are in good health, when our income is rising. It is easy to be a Christian at times like that.

The test of our faith is when the problems come and we are tempted to despair, to drift, and to throw out the things that are really important in life. Character is *revealed* in a crisis, not *made* in a crisis. Character is made in the day-by-day, mundane, trivial things of life — the routine. Character is developed there, but it is revealed when we get into a shipwreck, into a situation that threatens to swallow us up.

What should we do when things look as if they are falling apart and the ship is going to crash and disintegrate? What should we do when we are battered by big problems? Look what the sailors did: "Fearing that we would be dashed against the rocks, they dropped four anchors from the stern and prayed for daylight" (v. 29). The safest thing to do when we get in a storm is to drop our anchors. Just stand still. Situations change, and the sands of time shift. But the Bible says that those who put their trust in God are immovable like Mount Zion (Ps. 125:1).

Often when people encounter a major problem, they want to change everything else in their lives at the same time, because the situation feels overwhelming and they can't stand still. A person will lose his or her spouse by death or divorce, and the typical reaction is, "I'm going to quit my job. I'm going to sell everything and move to a whole new location and start over." But that is exactly what they *do not* need—more change. What they need to do is put down some anchors and get some stability.

Anchors for the Soul

Why was Paul so confident? Because he was encouraged by three tremendous truths, three foundational beliefs of the Christian life, that serve as anchors of the soul. These three truths can anchor you on the rock of stability, so that when the winds of crisis blow you back and forth, you will have confidence. These are truths that you can build your life on, that will stabilize you in the storm.

God's Presence

The first anchor in a crisis is *the presence of God*. In the midst of the storm Paul said, "Last night an angel of the God whose I am and whom I serve stood beside me and said, 'Do not be afraid, Paul'" (Acts 27:23–24). From this we learn that storms can never hide us from God. We may not see him, but he sees us. We may think God is a million miles away, but he is with us and is watching us. God sent a personal representative, an angel, to tell Paul, "I am with you. I see you in the stormy Mediterranean Sea in that little ship."

God promises in the Bible,

> "Never will I leave you; never will I forsake you" (Heb. 13:5).

> "Surely I am with you always" (Matt. 28:20).

> "I will ask the Father, and he will give you another Counselor to be with you forever" (John 14:16).

Over and over the Bible says that wherever we are, God is right there with us. We never go through anything by ourselves, because God is always with us. No matter what situation *you* are going through right now, God is with you. He is the anchor that you can fully trust.

God's Purpose

The second anchor in a crisis is found in Acts 27:24, where Paul quotes God's angel: "Do not be afraid, Paul. You must stand trial before Caesar; and God has graciously given you the lives of all who sail with you." God told Paul, "I have a plan for your life. You are on board this ship because I have a purpose for your being on this ship. I have a purpose for your life that is greater than the temporary storm you are in." The second anchor in a crisis is *God's purpose*.

Every Christian ought to have a sense of destiny. No person is born by accident, regardless of the circumstances of one's birth. You are not here on earth just to take up space; God has a specific purpose and plan for your life. Storms are simply temporary setbacks toward fulfilling that purpose. Absolutely nothing can change God's ultimate purpose for your life unless you choose to disobey him. If you choose to reject his plan, he will allow you to do that, but the Scriptures teach that no outside person can change God's plan for your life. God leaves that up to you. You can either accept it or you can reject it. No matter what happens on the outside, however, external forces cannot alter God's purpose for your life as long as you say, "God, I want to do your will."

God's purpose is greater than any situation you will ever experience. God has a plan beyond the problems you are facing right now. The point is this: It is dangerous to focus on your problems more than on your purpose for living. If you do that, you will start drifting and discarding. You will start despairing if you keep your eyes on the problem rather than on God's purpose for your life. Once you lose your goal, you will lose sight of the very meaning for which you exist, and you will become purposeless.

God's Promise

The third anchor that gives us confidence in a crisis is found in verse 25, where Paul says, "Keep up your courage, men, for I have faith in God that it will happen just as he told me." The third anchor is *God's promise*. God keeps his promises without fail. Storms cannot hide our faces from God, because God is always with us. Storms cannot change the purpose of God, because it is ultimate. Storms cannot destroy the child of God, because God's promise is sure.

Some of us are going through devastating crises right now. Our problems are overwhelming, and we think we are going under for the last time. God says this to you: You may lose the cargo; you may lose the tackle of the ship; you may lose the ship; you may even get wet—but you are going to make it because of the promise of God. As the old saying goes, "God said it, I believe it, and that settles it." So what do you do? Relax. Be confident in your crisis.

Pray While You Wait

What should we do while we are waiting for the crisis to end? The same thing the sailors did: "Fearing that we would be dashed against the rocks, they dropped four anchors from the stern and prayed for daylight" (Acts 27:29). *Anchor yourself on the truths of God and pray for daylight.*

What was the result aboard the ship? Morning came! When daylight came, the sailors didn't recognize the land, but they saw a bay with a sandy beach where they decided to run the ship aground. All 276 people jumped overboard and got safely to land (vv. 39–44).

In the storms of your life God says, "I am with you." Let his truth stabilize your life and give you the confidence you need in every crisis you face. Storms cannot hide God from you or you from God. You may be going through some difficult times right now, but God has a purpose for your life. There is a reason for it all, and you are going to make it safely to land!

PUTTING THOUGHTS INTO ACTION

1. What was one occasion when you made a decision more typical of the sailors than of the apostle Paul?

2. How have you experienced that first anchor—the presence of God—during a recent crisis?

CHAPTER 9

How Can I Ever Change?

If you could change one thing about yourself, what would it be? Most of us are interested in change. Bestseller lists perennially include self-help books, and the *New York Times* even has specific categories for Hardcover Advice and Softcover Advice books. We attend seminars and read books and try diets and listen to tapes.

Moreover, God wants us to change. A life that is never willing to change is a great tragedy—a wasted life. Change is a necessary part of a growing life, and we need change in order to remain fresh and to keep progressing.

But often the new ideas we gain from books or seminars just don't seem to last. Maybe we will be different for a while, but then discover that the new methods do not have a permanent effect. The main reason for this is that we work on the *exterior*, our outside behavior, instead of on the *interior*, our motives. Any lasting change must begin on the inside, and that is a work of God.

In the story of Jacob we can see the process God uses in helping us become the kind of person we have always wanted to be. The situation recorded in Genesis 32 was a turning point for Jacob and serves as a dramatic example of how God can change us.

THE FOUR-STEP PROCESS

Jacob was a somewhat shifty fellow. Even his name means "cheater" or "schemer" in Hebrew. But a life-changing experience transformed him into a new person, and he became Israel, the man after whom the entire nation of Israel was later named. After that experience Jacob was never the same again.

In this story we have a clear expression of the four-step process God uses to help us become the kind of people we want to be. It is a truly encouraging message — a message that says we don't have to stay in the rut we are in, that God will help us to change, to overcome that weakness or sore spot in our life. We just have to let him. So how do we let God do that?

Genesis 32 relates that while Jacob was alone one night, someone (an angel, according to Hosea 12:4) appeared and wrestled with him until daybreak.

> When the man [the angel] saw that he could not overpower him, he touched the socket of Jacob's hip so that his hip was wrenched as he wrestled with the man. Then the man said, "Let me go, for it is daybreak" (Gen. 32:25–26).

You may be asking, what does a wrestling match with an angel several thousand years ago have to do with changing me today? There are some important insights in this incident that show clearly the four steps required for transformation.

These four steps or phases are crisis, commitment, confession, and cooperation.

Crisis

The first step is *crisis.* Jacob had a long wrestling match with an angel, and the angel was struggling, but it was a no-win situation for them both. By daybreak the angel was getting tired of the struggle because he saw that he could not win. It was a situation beyond his control.

The lesson we see in this is that when God wants to change us, he starts by *getting our attention*, by putting us in a frustrating situation that is completely beyond our control. We cannot win, and we just keep getting more and more tired in the struggle. God uses experiences and problems and crises to get our attention. If we are experiencing a crisis right now, it is because God is getting ready to change us for the better. We never change until we get fed up with our current situation, until we get uncomfortable and discontented and start feeling miserable. When we become uncomfortable and miserable enough, we finally are motivated to let God do something in our lives.

A mother eagle will take the nest of her young and stir it up. She will make them uncomfortable and miserable, then kick them out and force them to learn to fly—for their own good in life. God does that in our lives: he makes us uncomfortable —if that's what it takes—because he knows what is best and he wants us to grow. He will allow a crisis, problem, irritation, or frustration in our lives to get our attention. He needs to do this because we won't change until our fear of change is exceeded by the pain we are experiencing.

Commitment

The second step in being changed by God is *commitment*. When the angel asked to be let go, Jacob replied, "I will not let you go unless you bless me" (v. 26). Jacob was committed; he was persistent; he stayed with the situation until he worked it out. He was in a situation he didn't like. It was frustrating and it was getting him down, but he was one hundred percent committed to staying with the situation until God turned it around for good.

Here is the lesson we learn from this: After God gets our attention with a problem, he does not solve it immediately. He waits a little longer to see whether we really mean business. Most people miss God's best for their lives because they give up too soon; they cop out; they become discouraged. When God allows a problem in their lives, instead of hanging in there and saying, "God, I'm not going to let go of this until you bless me, until you turn it around," they give up and end up missing God's best.

Often when people come to me for counseling, such as for marital conflict, I will ask, "Have you tried praying about the situation?"

They will reply, "Oh yes, I've prayed."

"How many times?"

"Once."

We are so conditioned to having instant everything—instant macaroni, instant access, instant success—that if we don't have an instant answer to our one prayer, or an instant turnaround, we say, "Forget it, God." Sometimes a couple struggling in their marriage are ready to give up just when success is around the corner. They are ready to cop out when the solution is almost there.

Even if we really want to change, we need to remember that we didn't get into our present mess overnight. Our attitudes and actions and habits and fears and weaknesses and ways of responding to our wife or husband took years to develop, and sometimes God has to remove them layer by layer. Usually it takes a while for God to change you.

It also takes time for us to adapt to the new conditions and situations. Psychologists tell us that it requires six weeks of doing something every day before something becomes a habit in our lives. This is why many people never get into the Bible. We read the Bible for two or three days, miss it for a few days, then read it again for a few days. We never get past that six-week barrier, and as a result, we never feel comfortable with it. We must do it every day for at least six weeks before we start becoming comfortable with this good, new habit.

Whatever you do, *don't give up*. There is hope. Hang in there. Be committed to getting God's best for your life.

Confession

The third step in being changed by God is *confession*. The angel asked Jacob, "What is your name?" And he answered, "Jacob" (v. 27). What was the purpose of the angel's question? It was to get Jacob to acknowledge his character by stating his name, which means "cheater" or "schemer." Jacob remembered the heartache he had caused by his scheming against his brother Esau, so when the angel asked, "What are you really like? What's your character?" Jacob's reply was saying, "I am a cheater. I am a schemer." Jacob admitted his weaknesses because even though he was a cheater and a schemer, he was also honest with himself. When he identified himself as "Jacob," he was admitting his character flaws.

This is an important part of God's process for changing us, because we never change until we honestly face and admit our faults, sins, weaknesses, and mistakes. God will not go to work on our problem until we first admit that we have a problem. We need to say, "Lord, I'm in a mess. I have a problem, and I admit I made it." Then God can go to work.

Have you ever noticed how easy it is to make excuses for our problems? We become experts at blaming other people and may say something like "It's not my fault, you know. It's really the environment I was brought up in—my parents caused it." Or we might say, "The situation I'm in right now is caused by my boss at work." Why do we act and talk this way? Because it is hard to admit fault in ourselves. And it can be scary to ask for help.

Why should we confess our faults to God—to let him know what's going on? No, he already knows. When we tell God we have sinned, it is no surprise to him; he knew our problems all along. We confess to him because he wants us to say, "You are right, God, I have a problem. I've blown it." It is humbling to admit our mistakes, but once we do, God gives us all his resources and power to help us change for the better. At this point we can start becoming the persons we have always wanted to be.

This event in Jacob's life was much more than just a wrestling match. It was an example of how God works in our own lives. First, he brings a frustrating crisis, like the wrestling match, in which we struggle with the situation. Second, we acknowledge, "It is obvious that I am not going to win. I can't get this situation under control—in my own power I am just going to keep on blowing it." Third, we need to continue. We need to commit ourselves to sticking with the situation and letting God work it out.

God will reply, "I am not going to bail you out right away, because I want to see if you really mean business. You said you wanted to change, so now I am going to allow the problem to stay just a little longer to see if you really mean business."

If we cop out at this point we will just encounter another problem of the same nature a little farther down the line. If we don't learn the lesson now, we will have to learn it later, because God is going to teach it to us one way or the other. We can save ourselves a lot of trouble by responding properly when the crisis first comes along.

Cooperation

The fourth step in being changed by God is *cooperation*. God began changing Jacob as soon as he admitted who he was and began to cooperate with God's plan. Jacob called the place where he wrestled with the angel "Peniel," meaning "the face of God" (Gen. 32:30). Jacob had come face to face with God. Every one of us must eventually come face to face with God, and when we do that, God can change us. God said to Jacob, "Now we can get down to business. I want you to relax. Just cooperate and trust me, and I will make the changes that you want made, and I will bless you." God didn't say, "Jacob, try real hard and use all your willpower to become perfect." That doesn't work, and God knows it. Willpower simply does not make permanent changes in our lives. That is attacking the *outward* circumstance. It is the *internal* motivation that makes the permanent changes, and that is what God works on.

When Jacob began to cooperate, God started working, and the first thing he did was give Jacob a new name, a new identity. God said, "Your name will no longer be Jacob, but Israel" (v. 28). After we have had a personal encounter with God, we can no longer be the same. God changed Jacob from a cheater and schemer to an Israel, a "prince of God." God knew Jacob's potential; he saw through Jacob's exterior of trying to be a worldly wise tough guy. God saw all of Jacob's weaknesses, but he also saw beneath the surface: "That's not the real you, Jacob. You're actually an Israel. You are a prince." God saw the prince in Jacob, and the former cheater began to become the man after whom the entire nation of Israel would be named.

LET GOD DO IT

God always knows how to bring out the best in your life, and he knows how to do it better than you do. If you let him, he will use whatever is necessary to accomplish this goal, because he doesn't want you to waste your life.

Do you want God's blessing on your life? Take the situation that is making you miserable right now, commit it to God, and say, "God, I am going to commit it to you. I am going to hold on to you until you turn this problem around for good." Then confess the errors that you need to confess, and cooperate with God.

Notice another detail in Jacob's story. The Bible says, "The sun rose above him as he passed Peniel, and he was limping because of his hip"

(v. 31). While they had been wrestling, the angel dislocated Jacob's hip, and as a result Jacob walked with a limp for the rest of his life. This is significant, because that thigh muscle is one of the most powerful muscles in the human body. When God had to get Jacob's attention, he touched him at a point of strength. When we start thinking, "This is what I am really good at, this is what I am really strong at," God may have to touch that very thing to get our attention. God touched Jacob's thigh, and it became a reminder to Jacob for the rest of his life that he was no longer to trust in his own power but in the power of God. He was no longer to live in his own strength but in God's strength, and in so doing he became a much stronger person.

Don't Run, But Stand

There is one more insight that comes from this incident in Jacob's life. Jacob often got himself into trouble because he was a cheater, and he often reaped what he sowed. But every time he got himself into a mess, he ran away from it. He just copped out. Finally, God said, "I know how to take care of that temptation—I'll put a limp in his walk." Never again could Jacob run away from a difficult situation. For the rest of his life he would have to stand and face his problems—not in his own strength but in God's strength. God often puts an obvious weakness in people whom he blesses, and often the weakness is some kind of physical problem. (There are other examples in the Bible of weaknesses like that, such as Paul's "thorn in the flesh"—2 Corinthians 12:7–10.)

What about you? How would you like to be permanently changed? What is the one thing you would most like to change about your life? Maybe it's a habit. Maybe it's a weakness. Maybe it's a character difficulty. Maybe it's something that has gotten you into more trouble than you could have imagined and now the situation is beyond your control. Maybe you are in a no-win situation that bothers you and bugs you and keeps you from developing the potential that God has given you.

Do you want God to change your life? He will—in his own way. He will use the processes of *crisis, commitment, confession,* and *cooperation.* And when he does the changing, it will become permanent. You will not have to worry about your willpower and staying with it because you will be cooperating with God, relaxing and trusting him.

Maybe you have been limiting God by making excuses, blaming other people, or rationalizing. It is hard to drop your mask and say, "God, I have a weakness. I have a problem." Until you do this, things will just stay the same as they are now. When you do this, you are changed for the rest of your life.

The good news is this: Beneath all those things you know about yourself that you do not like, God sees an Israel. He sees the prince or princess in your life. He sees what you can become. He sees your potential, and he wants to change you from a Jacob to an Israel. Let God do his changing!

PUTTING THOUGHTS INTO ACTION

1. What is the one thing you would most like to change about your life?
2. Think through each step in the change process and how you can apply it to your current situation.

CHAPTER 10

How Did I Get Myself into This Mess?

Samson was a ruler in Israel for twenty years. His story is told at length in Judges 13–16. It began strikingly, with an angel's announcement to his sterile parents that they would, miraculously, have a son and that he would become a judge in Israel. After Samson grew up, he was indeed a judge in Israel for twenty years. The term "judge" did not mean then what it means today; Samson was a military leader and tribal chieftain. The Israelites' main enemy at that time was the Philistines.

This leader had everything going for him: supernatural strength, good looks, and a relationship with God. Yet, in spite of that, he was his own worst enemy. He wasted his life and brought all kinds of troubles on himself.

Unfortunately, human nature is universal, and we today can fall into the same kinds of traps as Samson. Samson made a mess of his life because he made three fatal choices and didn't learn from his mistakes. He typified three of the most common ways that we bring troubles on ourselves. If we can identify these three traps, we can work out the problems we are in right now and avoid some problems in the future.

LEARNING FROM OUR MISTAKES

First, we are *asking for trouble if we refuse to learn from our mistakes*. Samson had two big weaknesses in his life, and he never learned to control either of them. All of his life they plagued him, and later they caused his downfall. The first weakness was a bad temper. Samson often got angry; he frequently blew up. A primary motive for his actions was revenge. Samson killed thirty men to get their clothes because he burned with anger (Judg. 14:12–19). He set a field afire just to get even (15:3–5). He said to a group of men he didn't like, "Since you've acted like this, I won't stop until I get my revenge on you" (v. 7). Later he said, "I merely did to them what they did to me" (v. 11). And then he killed another thousand men.

The other weakness was uncontrolled physical desire. He was physically strong but morally weak. He deliberately ignored God's principles; his life was really a pathetic cycle of failures. He never learned; he kept making the same mistakes over and over again. For him it was really kind of a game: "How close to the fire can I get and not get burned?"

Samson played this kind of game with Delilah, a Philistine prostitute. She kept asking the source of his strength and kept getting teased by Samson, but each time she got a little closer to the truth. He was playing with temptation as he toyed with her, and soon he got burned. But we tend to do the same thing. We say things like "Just this one time" to allow ourselves guilty pleasures. "What's one time going to hurt, anyway? Just this one time I'm going to worry; just this one time I'm going to get depressed; just this one time I'm going to try this or that." None of us plans to be a failure—it just comes on us naturally. And gradually. It is a step-by-step process, as little by little we become weakened. Our whole lives do not fall apart in one day; the problem builds up over a period of time as we refuse to learn from our mistakes.

You may be saying, "But this is an area of my life that I have no control over. I am defeated in it over and over again. It is a chronic area of failure in my life, and I just don't know how to overcome it. That's just the way I am."

The good news is that God says, "I will give you the power to break out of that cycle of failure." When Samson finally faced the facts, God broke his cycle of failure, gave him the power to do what he should do, and gave him victory. God will do that for us when we face the facts.

CHOOSING OUR FRIENDS

The second principle we learn from Samson's life is that *we are asking for trouble if we choose the wrong friends.* Somebody has wisely said, "If you want to soar with the eagles, you can't run with the turkeys." You will eventually become like the people you spend the most time with. That is why it is important to choose your friends wisely. Samson was defeated by bad associations; even though God had chosen him for a special task, he developed unhealthy relationships, and his friends led him astray.

God has a special purpose for each of us, but we get ourselves into trouble when we choose the wrong friends. Here is a challenging question: Do your friends keep you from living a hundred percent for God? Do they tear you down, or do they build you up? Do you find yourself having to conform to things you don't like to do? The book of Proverbs warns us over and over again about negative associations. Constant exposure to wrong attitudes and wrong values will eventually take its toll in our lives. It is always easier to pull someone down than it is to lift him up.

What kind of friends should you have? The kind who bring out the best in you, who lift you up, who encourage you, who make you a better person.

TAKING GOD SERIOUSLY

There is a third principle in Samson's story, and this is really the most important one of all, because we see it throughout his life: *We are asking for trouble when we refuse to take God seriously.* Samson was careless about his spiritual life. He never did get really serious with God, and this problem showed up in more than one way.

In the first place, Samson was always doing his own thing. He lived for himself. His was basically a very selfish lifestyle, and he let his personal desires dictate his actions. Samson lived by the philosophy, "If it feels good, do it." God's plan for Samson was greatness, and that is God's plan for you. He has a purpose for your life; you were not put here on earth by accident. But Samson's pattern was carelessness; he just kind of took things for granted and never really was serious, and the result was uselessness in his life. After twenty years as a judge, Samson still had not restrained the Philistines, and in the end they did him in.

Another sign that Samson refused to take God seriously is that from all appearances he never prayed about anything, except before his final act, when he brought the house down (Judg. 16:28–30). He was impulsive; he was impetuous. He did not ask God for direction. He just went ahead and did whatever he wanted to do.

We would save ourselves many problems and spare ourselves much pain if we would just stop and ask God for direction before we jump into something with both feet and get all messed up. Samson turned to God only when he got into a jam. That is what we call "foxhole Christianity": "Lord, if you will just get me out of this dilemma, I promise I will live for you from now on."

To many people, God is just kind of an afterthought, a convenience. When things get tough and tight, they turn to him in desperation. But when everything is all right, they ignore him. Taking God seriously means paying attention to what he says and seeking his guidance and wisdom every day.

Samson never really got serious about living for God until the very end of his life, after everything had finally fallen apart: he was captured by the Philistines, they gouged out his eyes, and they made him grind grain at a mill, a job normally reserved for animals.

Notice what happened after everything collapsed: Samson finally prayed (16:28). I wonder what kind of history Samson would have had if he had prayed right from the beginning. Why did he have to wait until everything fell apart before he finally turned to God? The result of Samson's prayerlessness was that he completely lost his potential in life. He was discredited and lost his freedom; he became a slave to the people he had been sent to conquer. Samson truly reaped what he had sowed.

GOD NEVER GIVES UP

This would be a hopelessly tragic story if it just ended there—but it doesn't. The Philistines had cut off Samson's hair, which was a sign of the covenant he had made with the Lord. Samson's hair was just an outward symbol; it was not the *source* of his strength, but the *sign* of his strength. When the Philistines shaved his head, it is as if they were saying, "Samson, we are changing on the outside what has already been cut off in your heart. You are not really serious about your commitment to the Lord."

But notice that "the hair on his head began to grow again after it had been shaved" (Judg. 16:22). The process of renewal was starting. Samson repented and began to pray. As he began to look to God for strength, God honored his desire. God gave him his strength back, and Samson ended his life with an inspiring act of heroism.

Samson was brought to the great temple of the false god Dagon so that thousands of his enemies could laugh and joke about him and also about his god—the true God of Israel. Samson was placed between the two main pillars of the temple, and with every last ounce of strength God gave him—in answer to prayer—he pushed the columns aside, and the roof of the huge building collapsed, killing everybody inside the temple and the three thousand people on the roof. God had sent Samson to conquer this enemy nation in the first place, and now God was able to accomplish more through Samson in his death than during his life. That is a sad statement on Samson's life, but he finally did defeat the enemy. When God gave him a second chance, Samson had the greatest victory at the end of his life.

In a sense this is a comforting fact. Maybe you feel that you have messed up your life so badly that God will never love you and use you again—but remember Samson. God never gave up on Samson, and he has not given up on you. God sees your potential, and he remembers why he made you: you were created for great things. Only as you move into the center of God's will can you discover why you were made. But when you do, things will begin to click and fall into place. You will feel fulfilled and will become successful in God's sight as you realize that you are doing what God created you to do.

THE COMFORT OF GOD'S GRACE

There is something very encouraging about Samson: he is included in God's Hall of Fame, the panorama of people of great faith displayed in Hebrews 11! Why? Because God could take a person who was a total failure in different areas of his life and still use him for good and great things. If God only used people who were perfect, nothing would ever get done. Instead, he uses ordinary people, who have imperfections and weaknesses and may even fail in a big way.

What should you do if you are a Samson? Exactly what Samson finally did: turn your life over to the Lord. Give him all the pieces, and let him say to you, "I will give you the power to break loose from those things that are tying you down and causing your hang-ups and preventing me from working in your life." Only God knows the greatness and potential in your life, and you will never bring it out on your own. God must do it in his strength. Let him start today!

Putting Thoughts into Action

1. Which of Samson's mistakes do you identify with the most right now?
2. How do you plan to follow up on God's offer of a second chance?

CHAPTER 11

How Can I Overcome Loneliness?

Loneliness is one of the most miserable feelings a person can experience. Sometimes you may feel that nobody loves you, that nobody even cares if you exist. You do not even have to be alone to feel lonely; you can feel lonely in a crowd. It is not the number of people around you that determines your loneliness; it is your relationship to them. In the urban world that we now live in, people have never lived closer together, and yet they have never felt farther apart.

Can you be wealthy and lonely? Ask the late aviation and movie tycoon Howard Hughes. Can you be beautiful and lonely? Ask the late actress

Marilyn Monroe. Can you be married and lonely? Ask the people who marry because of loneliness and then get divorced a few years later for the same reason.

Everyone experiences loneliness at one time or another, but there are distinct causes and distinct cures for it. Sometimes we bring loneliness on ourselves, but other times we find ourselves in situations that are inevitable and uncontrollable. That is the condition in which the apostle Paul found himself as he wrote his second letter to Timothy. Paul was a dying old man as he wrote from a prison in Rome to his good friend Timothy and urged the younger man to visit him because he was lonely.

WHAT CAUSES LONELINESS

There are four basic causes of loneliness.

Transition

The first cause is *the transitions of life*. Life is full of transitions and stages. Growing older is a series of changes, and any change can produce loneliness. You are lonely when you are born, and you cry until you are cuddled. The first school you went to was a lonely experience. Getting a job is lonely. Changing jobs is lonely. Retiring is lonely. The death of a loved one is lonely.

Any new experience we have to deal with can be lonely. To make things worse, we tend to isolate people who are dying. Seventy percent of people in rest homes never get a visit from anybody!

Paul was in the final transition of life, and he knew that his time was short—and he was lonely. He said, "I am already being poured out like a drink offering, and the time has come for my departure" (2 Tim. 4:6). He was saying, in effect, "My time is short. I know it. I may be martyred by Nero very quickly. If not, I will die just from old age." As Paul spent his last days alone, he wrote, "I have fought the good fight. I have finished the race. I have kept the faith. Now there is in store for me the crown of righteousness" (vv. 7–8).

Separation

The second basic cause of loneliness is *separation*. Being isolated—apart from your friends, apart from your family (because of career or military service or something else)—causes loneliness.

Solitary confinement is the most devastating form of punishment, because people need people. We need interaction; we need acceptance.

Paul wrote to Timothy from prison, "Do your best to come to me quickly" (v. 9). Then Paul mentioned his best friends, but none of them were with him except Luke. Paul was in prison in a foreign country, and he told Timothy, "I miss these people." These were Paul's best friends, his previous traveling companions. Paul was a "people person"; he loved to be among people, and he never went anywhere alone. But now, at the end of his life, he was experiencing the loneliness of separation because his friends were in other countries.

Today you can just pick up a phone and call someone, but in those days Paul couldn't just "reach out and touch someone," as the famous AT&T ad put it. It took a long time to get in contact with somebody.

Twice in this passage (vv. 9, 13) Paul asked Timothy to "Come," and then he said, "Do your best to get here before winter" (v. 21). Why did he say this? Because time was running out. He was saying, "Timothy, I may not be around much longer. And I really want to see you. Come back and see me."

Whom do you need to call? Whom do you need to write a letter of appreciation to? You need to do it now, while there is still time. You can help relieve someone's loneliness of separation by making that contact you have been putting off.

Opposition

The third basic cause of loneliness is *opposition*. Paul says, "Alexander the metalworker did me a great deal of harm" (v. 14). In other words, "Not only am I getting old and sitting here alone in prison, but I have been attacked." We don't know what Alexander had done to Paul. Maybe he slandered Paul's name or attacked his reputation. Maybe he was turning people against Paul.

Some of the meanest things can be said by children on the playground. Do you remember when you were a little kid and everybody ganged up on you? All of a sudden during one recess the fickle finger of popularity turned, and everyone was against you: "You're not our friend anymore!" You felt opposed, and you felt alone. It is a lonely feeling to go through a painful experience like this, to suffer rejection while everyone else is having fun. It is a lonely feeling to be misunderstood, to be embarrassed, to be humiliated. The temptation when this happens is to draw yourself into your shell and build up walls. But doing that only makes you lonelier.

Rejection

The fourth basic cause of loneliness is the most serious one in that it causes the most pain. It is the loneliness of *rejection*. It is when you feel as though you have been betrayed or forsaken—abandoned in your time of need by those closest to you.

Paul felt this way; he felt deserted. He said of his trial before Nero, "At my first defense, no one came to my support, but everyone deserted me" (v. 16). You can almost hear the pain in Paul's voice: "When things got tough, everybody left me. When the trial warmed up, nobody was there." Nobody spoke for his defense; everybody copped out.

Rejection is one of the most difficult things for a human being to handle. That is why divorce is so painful, and that is why God hates adultery: it is a betrayal, and it hurts lives. It is an act of unfaithfulness, an abandoning, a forsaking, and it is a very painful experience. God says that every human being has an emotional need for acceptance, and when that need is violated, it is a serious sin.

Dealing with Loneliness

There are both good ways and self-defeating ways to deal with loneliness. One self-defeating way is to become a workaholic. You spend all your time and energy working, working, working. You get up in the morning and work all day until finally you flop into bed exhausted at night. But eventually that takes its toll on you physically and emotionally.

Some people try materialism: they buy everything they can. "If I can just get a lot of things around me, I will be happy." But things do not satisfy. If you were put on an island and told, "You can have anything you want except human contact," how long do you think you would be happy? Not very long, because things do not satisfy. You can't purchase happiness.

Some people have an extramarital affair because of loneliness. Others turn to alcohol or drugs. Some people do nothing—they just sit around and hold a pity party.

So what did Paul do? Paul did four things to combat his loneliness, and they are just as appropriate today as they were when he went through his days of loneliness. The four things for getting through those times are *utilize, minimize, recognize,* and *empathize.*

Utilize

The first way to deal with loneliness is to *utilize your time wisely.* In other words, make the best of your bad situation. Resist the temptation to do nothing. Loneliness has a tendency to paralyze you if you just sit around and do nothing. Resist that—think of a creative way to take advantage of your lack of distractions.

As the saying goes, "If life gives you a lemon, make lemonade." Whatever you can do to combat loneliness, do it. This is what Paul did: "I sent Tychicus to Ephesus" (2 Tim. 4:12), and "When you come, bring the cloak that I left with Carpus at Troas, and my scrolls, especially the parchments" (v. 13). Paul refused to sit around and mope. He did not say, "Poor me, poor me." He did not complain, "God, is this what I get for thirty years of ministry? Is this my reward for starting lots of churches, for being the person most responsible for the spread of Christianity in the Roman world? Is this what I get—to die in loneliness in a damp prison in Rome?"

No pity party for Paul! Instead, he said, "If I am going to be lonely, I may as well be comfortable. I am going to make the best of a bad situation. Bring my coat so at least I will be warm."

Often lonely people do not take care of themselves. They do not eat right, they do not exercise, and they ignore their personal needs. But Paul said, "Bring my coat and my books, and I will capitalize on this lack of interruption; I will use it for writing and study time." This was a great change of gears for Paul, because he was an activist, a church planter. More than anything else, he wanted to be in the Colosseum preaching instead of in a prison studying. But sometimes God can use loneliness for good. If Paul had been in the Colosseum, he would have been preaching, but

God left him in prison and we got part of the New Testament instead!

Probably the only way that God could get Paul to sit still was to put him in prison. And Paul's response was, "If I cannot be where the action is, I will create action right here."

Minimize

The second way to deal with loneliness is to *minimize the hurt*. Play down the loneliness. Do not exaggerate it or rehearse it over and over. Do not allow the loneliness to make you bitter, and do not allow resentment to build up in your life. Paul said, "No one came to my support, but ... may it not be held against them" (v. 16).

Paul had much time on his hands, but one thing he didn't have any time for was to become resentful. He knew that resentment would only make him lonelier and build a wall around his life. Resentment locks us in a self-imposed prison and drives people away, because nobody likes to be around a cynic—a person who is always bitter and complaining. Paul said, "I want to be a better person, not a bitter person, so I will utilize my time and minimize my hurt."

Recognize

The third way to deal with loneliness is to *recognize God's presence*. Paul said, "The Lord stood at my side and gave me strength" (v. 17). Where is God when you are lonely? He is right next to you. Jesus said, "I will not leave you as orphans" (John 14:18)—"I will not leave you comfortless" (KJV). God said, "Never will I leave you; never will I forsake you" (Heb. 13:5).

There is no place where God is not. He is everywhere at all times, and you can constantly talk with him. As long as you understand this, you are never really alone. Prayer is a fantastic tool that you can use in lonely times. Talk to God, and let him speak to you. David learned that fellowship with God is a tremendous antidote to loneliness. He would cry out, "God, I'm so lonely! King Saul is chasing me, and I am alone in a cave. But then I turn my thoughts to you. Where can I get away from your presence? If I go up to heaven, you are there. Anywhere on earth, you are there. I can't get away from you" (Ps. 139:7–8 paraphrased). David learned that loneliness is a signal that it is time for us to become better acquainted with God.

Singer Amy Grant recorded a great song that goes, "I love a lonely day. It makes me think of you.... It chases me to you. It clears my heart." In effect, she is saying, "It gives me a chance to really focus on you, God." So what should you do? Do what Paul did. Don't mope around; don't give in to the temptation to do nothing. Focus on God. Make your time count.

Empathize

The fourth way to deal with loneliness is to *empathize with other people's needs.* Instead of focusing inward on yourself, focus outward on other people. Instead of looking at yourself, look out to other people. Start helping other lonely people. That is what Paul did. His whole goal in life was an outgoing ministry—serving others without focusing on himself. As he said, "The Lord stood at my side and gave me strength, so that through me the message might be fully proclaimed and all the Gentiles might hear it" (2 Tim. 4:17). Paul was lonely and at the end of his life, yet he never forgot his life's goal: to help other people.

When Corrie ten Boom was a young woman in the Netherlands, she fell head over heels in love with a young man. But he broke off the relationship and married one of her good friends. Corrie was devastated. Nothing hurts more than being rejected and having somebody else chosen over you. When Corrie got home, her dad said something very wise to her: "Corrie, your love has been blocked, and he has married somebody else. Now, there are two things you can do with a blocked love. You can dam it up inside and hold it all inside and it will eat you up—or you can rechannel it to something or someone else and can focus on other people's needs. You can live a life of love, meeting other people's needs." Corrie chose to do the latter, as we know from her captivating book *The Hiding Place*.

Consider the couple in agony who really want children but can't have them. What are they going to do with that love that they would have had for their children? They can hold it in, or they can rechannel it. There are many children in the world who need love. This couple can focus on the needs of others.

We need to stop building walls between us and others and start building bridges. We need to stop complaining, "God, I'm so lonely," and start saying, "God, help me be a friend to somebody today. Help me build a bridge instead of building a wall."

Love is the antidote to loneliness. Instead of waiting to be loved, we need to give love; then love will be given back to us in abundant measure.

FILLING THE VACUUM

What does God have to say about your loneliness? What does he offer to fill the vacuum? The first thing he says is, "I understand. I really understand." The Son of God knows what it is like to be lonely. In Jesus' darkest hour—the night before he was crucified on the cross—he was in the Garden of Gethsemane and all his friends fell asleep. When the soldiers came and took him to the trial, all his disciples fled. Then Peter denied him three times. When Jesus took the sins of the world on himself on the cross, he cried out, "My God, my God, why have you forsaken me?" (Mark 15:34).

Jesus understands loneliness. He says to you, "I understand how you feel. I care about you, and I want to help you." Let him help you conquer your loneliness as you turn to him in prayer and reach out in love to lonely people around you.

Putting Thoughts into Action

1. What was a lonely situation for you, and how did you overcome it?
2. Think of one person in your church or neighborhood or workplace whom you know feels lonely, and consider some specific way to help him or her dispel that loneliness.

CHAPTER 12

WHY IS THIS HAPPENING TO ME?

How should we respond when other people cause us trouble? When family rejects us? When a good friend double-crosses us? When a colleague at work lies about us? A prime example of suffering from the troubles brought on by other people is Joseph of the Old Testament, whose story is told in Genesis 37–50.

Joseph was the second-youngest of twelve brothers. There was a lot of sibling rivalry in the family, and the older brothers began to get especially jealous of Joseph because of their father's favoritism toward him. When the problem came to a head, the brothers threw Joseph into a pit and left him there to die. But some traveling merchants came by, and the brothers said, "Let's just sell him instead of killing him." So Joseph's older brothers sold him to these foreign merchants, who took him as a slave to Egypt.

So Joseph found himself in a foreign country. He did not know anyone, he could not speak the language at first, and he was enslaved against his will. On top of that, his master's wife decided to seduce him one day. After he refused, she falsely accused him of rape, and he was thrown into prison. He was lonely and hurting, and he had every right to ask, "Why me?"

But notice Joseph's attitude as he talked with his brothers many years after these terrible things happened. Reflecting on those events, he said, "You intended to harm me, but God intended it for good to accomplish what is now being done, the saving of many lives" (Gen. 50:20). In other words, "You meant this for bad, but God turned it around and used it for good in my life, in your lives, and in the lives of many other people."

Learning What Joseph Knew

Why was Joseph able to hang in there? Because of three important truths that he recognized in his life. These truths helped him endure tragic situations and overcome adversity.

First, Joseph knew that *God sees everything we go through, and he cares.* This is very evident in Joseph's life. He never doubted that God saw what was going on in his life and cared about it. There is an important phrase that is found five times in the story of Joseph, each time after a major crisis or defeat: "But the Lord was with Joseph" (for example, Gen. 39:21). Even when everything was going wrong, the Lord was still with Joseph.

The second thing Joseph recognized is that *God has given everyone freedom of choice.* You are not a puppet or a robot that says little prayers to God and is controlled by him. God gave all of us freedom of choice, and when we choose to ignore what is right, God does not force his will on us. It is often the case that when we bring a problem on ourselves, we blame God as if it were *his* fault. God gets blamed for many things he never caused. When we see a major accident

183

or tragedy or problem or crisis, we try to sound spiritual by saying, "It must be God's will"—as if God gets enjoyment out of planning mistakes and heartaches!

The fact of the matter is that God's will is *not* always done. God has a will for our lives, but he has given us a free will too. When we choose to go our own way, he chooses to limit himself. He will allow us the freedom of choice to make mistakes and cause problems in our own lives. And because everyone else also has free choice, the mistakes and decisions other people make can hurt us. Joseph's brothers willfully chose to plot against him. This was a sin, but God allowed it because he didn't make people to be puppets.

The third truth Joseph recognized is that *God is in ultimate control of the final outcome.* He can take all our mistakes and all the sins that other people commit against us, then turn them around and bring good out of the bad. Even though we may lose a battle here and there, God has already won the war. God will take even very bad circumstances and turn them around for us. When we think everything is falling apart in our lives, God has the final say. He decides what is going to happen with the messes we face.

Consider Joseph. He was nearly killed, was sold into slavery, was accused of rape, and then was put into prison. His life was moving steadily downhill. But then God took these tragedies, turned them around, and out of them brought much good. While Joseph was in prison, he made friends with the right-hand man of Pharaoh. When this man was restored to power, he learned of Pharaoh's dreams and remembered that Joseph could interpret dreams. Joseph was brought out of prison and invited to the Pharaoh's palace to interpret the dream. He said, "Pharaoh, God is telling you that you are going to have seven years of good crops and then seven years of famine, so you need to prepare for this."

Pharaoh was so impressed with Joseph that he made him second in command over all of Egypt. Joseph went from a foreign slave in prison to the second-greatest leader in Egypt, and by so doing he saved Egypt plus several other nations, including Israel, from starvation.

God sees what is going on, but he also has given us a free choice, and he does not intervene against our free will. He has limited himself. But he will use our bad choices, and even the bad things that happen to us, to turn things around and bring good out of them in the final outcome—if we let him. That is, if we trust in him no matter what our circumstances are. This is why Joseph could say at the end of his life, "You meant it for harm, but God meant it for good." The only way God could bring good out of this was for Joseph to hang on, even when he did not understand it all.

COPING WITH ADVERSITY

Perhaps you are going through a trial right now. Maybe you are an innocent party and the victim of a situation that you didn't cause. Consider Joseph's reaction. The first thing he did *not* do was to give in to self-pity. If you are in a problem or trial right now, you cannot afford self-pity. That is one of the major causes of depression. Usually when we are in a serious problem and our self-esteem is already at a low ebb, we start condemning ourselves and putting ourselves down, and we end up holding a pity party for ourselves.

Joseph did not do that; he did not blame himself. The crisis he was in was not his fault, and he tried to look at the situation realistically. When a boat is facing a storm, the way to make it is to face the wind head-on. If you let the boat turn sideways, the storm will capsize it. When storms come into our lives, the best way to overcome them is to face them head-on—as Joseph did.

If you are in a period of discouragement because you are going through a trial and you are asking yourself, "Why is this happening to me?" consider this: *Never make a major decision when you are depressed*. Often, when we get discouraged, we are tempted to say, "I'm just going to quit" or "I'm going to move" or "I'm going to change jobs" or "I'm going to file for divorce." Never make a major decision when you are depressed, because at that time your feelings are unreliable and you cannot exercise accurate judgment. Your focus is blurry, and your perspective is distorted. Instead, face the storm head-on and don't get involved in self-pity.

There is another trait we see in Joseph's life when all those things were going wrong: he didn't give in to bitterness. After many years Joseph met his brothers again because they had to go to Egypt for grain. As they entered Joseph's presence, bowing before the second in command over Egypt, they failed to recognize him as their younger brother.

When Joseph tried to tell them who he was, they were both shocked and scared. Here was a brother they had tried to kill years earlier, and now he was in a position to control them and do as he wished with them. But Joseph forgave them. Joseph knew that *you cannot afford the excess baggage of bitterness in your life.*

What should we do when we are tempted to be bitter? *Turn it over to the Lord.* That's what Joseph did: he maintained his faith and hope in God, he believed that things would work out well in the end, and he kept on with his spiritual life.

When things go wrong, we may reject the Person we need the most—the Lord. When a problem comes into your life, you may say, "God, why did you allow this to happen?" You may rebel against God as if it were his fault. Instead, you should say, "Lord, take this problem." God can take situations that are totally bad and turn them around. When people use situations to try to destroy you, God can use them to develop you. He loves to turn crucifixions into resurrections.

GAINING STRENGTH FOR A CRISIS

The Bible gives us not only answers to the reasons for suffering, but also some practical help and comfort when we are experiencing suffering. If we will apply the following sources of strength to our life, no situation can devastate us, and no crisis can tear us apart permanently.

The Plan of God

The first source of strength that we see in Joseph's life is *the plan of God*: "In all things God works for the good of those who love him, who have been called according to his purpose" (Rom. 8:28). This verse does not say that everything is good; there is a lot of evil in this world, and God's will is not always done. But it says that in the life of a

Christian, God makes all things—even the bad things—work out for good.

God has not rejected you; he has your best interests at heart. He will take the situation you are going through, even if it is a terrible one, and use it for a good overall purpose in your life. He will bring out greater glory in the long run. God is greater than any problem you will ever face. Of course, it is difficult to see how God is working in a bad situation while you are in it. But later, as you look back, your perspective is better and you can see what God was doing and how he used this situation in a great and purposeful way in your life.

When you understand this truth, you can look back and say to people who give you a hard time, "You meant it for bad, but God meant it for good. You meant it to destroy me, but God used it to develop me. You meant it to tear me down, but God used it to make me a stronger and more mature person." No matter what happens—even though you lose a battle—the war has been won and the final outcome is in God's hand. He will turn failures around and bring good out of them if you give him the opportunity.

The Promises of God

A second source of strength when we are going through a crisis is *the promises of God*. There are more than seven thousand promises of God in the Bible, and we need to start claiming them. They are like blank checks; they need to be used.

I suggest that you pick out a few verses, write them down on some little cards, carry them in your pocket, and memorize them. One man put verses on cards and stuck them on his car's sun visor. At every stoplight he would flip the visor down and read a verse, and when the light turned green, he would flip it back up. He has memorized hundreds of verses just while idling at stoplights, never spending any extra time. You might put some verses on your bathroom mirror and memorize them while you are shaving your beard or blow-drying your hair. The promises of God give us hope, and they give us strength and comfort.

The Scriptures claim that they were written to encourage us and give us hope (Rom. 15:4). What we need to do is read God's promises, memorize them, and then claim them in faith.

The People of God

There is a third source of strength that should help us when we have to go through a crisis: *the people of God*. Every church ought to be a caring community of individuals where the people love each other, support each other, pray for each other, laugh together, cry together, and carry burdens together. We need one another; God meant for the church to be a strong support system as we encourage and help each other.

But it can't be a support system if we don't know each other. We need to get involved in some kind of small group Bible study in the church. We need to find a small group of people with whom we can meet on a regular basis and then share our lives with them and pray with them. As we do this, we will discover that there are other people who have the same problems we do and therefore can encourage us. There will be people who have had our same or similar problems and are now on the other end; they have been through the tunnel, so they can now reach in and help pull us through.

The Bible says that God often allows us to go through intense trials and problems and then comforts us so that we in turn may offer comfort to others in similar situations (2 Cor. 1:3–4). God uses us in that way; he usually works on people through other people.

The Presence of Christ

The fourth source of strength in a crisis is the greatest of all: *the presence of God in Jesus Christ*. The Bible says that Jesus Christ is God's Son, that he is alive today, and that you can have a personal relationship with him. There are literally millions of people around the world who are living proof of this. The presence of Christ can help us through any situation.

Joseph was an example in the Old Testament of what Jesus did in the New Testament: they both suffered for the benefit of other people. Joseph suffered so that in the long run, when the famine came to the Middle East, his policies of food storage would save thousands of people from starvation. That is a picture of what Jesus Christ did.

Even though he was perfect and blameless, Jesus died on the cross to save us from the terrible consequences of sin.

God has given each of us a free will, so he could not force his will on us without making us puppets or robots. We live in a world in which people sin and hurt each other. When we give our lives to Christ and trust him, he sees us through each situation and gives us the ability to see how he is going to bring it all together in the end. The cross is the ultimate example of people planning things for evil but God working them out for good and for the blessing of mankind.

Perhaps you have been hurt deeply by a family member, as Joseph was—perhaps a brother, sister, parent, husband, wife—or by a boyfriend or girlfriend. If so, do what Joseph did: Don't give in to self-pity or bitterness. Instead, *take all the pieces and turn them over to Jesus Christ.* Let him bring something new and refreshing and beautiful out of that ugly situation.

But you may be thinking, "It's just not fair. I don't deserve this." Or maybe you have a friend who is in trouble, and you say, "It's just not fair that that happened."

And I reply, you are exactly right. There are many unfair things happening in this world. And that is why one day at the end of time the Bible says God is going to settle the score. There will be a judgment day, when all of the hurt inflicted on innocent people will be corrected and justified. God is going to settle the score at the end of time. But for now our duty is to keep on keeping on and see what God can do in our own lives for our development instead of letting the unfair things devastate us.

So if you are going through a situation where you are tempted to ask, "Why is this happening to me?" realize that God is looking on and that wrong hurts him. He has also given you a free will and allows everyone the freedom to choose. So turn to the plan of God and see that he will turn around even an ugly situation and use it for good if you will let him. Turn to the plan of God and take hope in what lies ahead. Turn to the promises of God and rely on them. Turn to the people of God and get involved in a warm church where you can have your needs met and can be used to meet the needs of others.

Most important, turn to the presence of Christ and let him into your life. Out of the worst, God can bring the best. That is the message of this story. Many Christians can look at their past and say, "That is so true. Everything had fallen apart in my life, and then I gave my life to Christ and he began to put it back together." Turning your life over to Jesus Christ does not mean that he will always take you out of the storm, but it does mean that he will give you the courage and the strength to weather it. All things do not work together for good for everybody in this world. They will only work together for good if we give God the pieces and give him our lives, and then he works things out for good. But as long as you hold back, he doesn't work things out for your good.

So you need to believe in Christ; you need to be a Christian, what the Bible calls "born again." What does that mean? You do two things, stated in two simple words. One word is *repent*, and the other word is *believe*. "Repent" means to change: change the way you think about God and your sin.

It leads to turning away from darkness and turning to light, turning away from guilt to forgiveness, turning away from selfishness and turning toward God. And then you "believe." You believe that God's Son can forgive your sin, that he can make your life better, that he wants to work in your life; that he has a plan for you, and that he can take all the messes and bad situations—even your irritations—and turn them around and use them for good—if you will let him. If you do that, you will be able to say as you look back, "They meant it for bad when they were really sticking it to me, but God meant it for good. God used the bad things in my life. He used them to develop me and make me a better person, and I am thankful for it."

PUTTING THOUGHTS INTO ACTION

1. Describe an incident in your life that, amid its tragic circumstances, resulted in some good, for you or for others.
2. Give some examples of how one or more of God's sources of strength have been demonstrated in your life.

197

We want to hear from you. Please send your comments about this book to us in care of zreview@zondervan.com. Thank you.

GRAND RAPIDS, MICHIGAN 49530 USA

ZONDERVAN.COM/
AUTHORTRACKER